## GUINNESS FACTBOOK

# RAIL

GUINNESS FACTBOOK

# RAIL

## John Marshall

**GUINNESS
BOOKS**

Editor: Beatrice Frei
Design and Layout: Alan Hamp

Published in Great Britain by Guinness
Superlatives Ltd,
2 Cecil Court, London Road, Enfield, Middlesex.

Typeset by MS Filmsetting Limited, Frome,
Somerset
Printed in Great Britain by Dotesios Printers Ltd,
Bradford-on-Avon, Wiltshire

British Library Cataloguing in Publication Data

Marshall, John, *1922–May 1–*
    Rail.——(Guinness factbook)
    1. Railroads——History
    I. Title
    385'.09      TF15

ISBN 0–85112–403–8

*Frontispiece*
The observation car at the rear of the east-bound *Canadian* in the Lower Kicking
Horse Canyon, British Columbia, Canadian Pacific Railway. (Canadian Pacific)

*Cover Illustration*
The Great Western Railway 4–4–0 *City of Truro*, the first locomotive to travel
over 100 mph (161 km/h). (John Marshall)

# Contents

George Stephenson's *Invicta*, built in 1830 for the Canterbury & Whitstable Railway. (The Science Museum, London)

# Introduction

This book is intended as a handy reference work, providing data about British and various foreign railways. It is not an abridged version of *The Guinness Book of Rail Facts and Feats* which does not contain most of the material in this Factbook. The author hopes that it may find use as a work of reference for railway historians.

The selection of this raw material of history may appear arbitrary, particularly that of the French National Railways (SNCF) as the only example out of over 20 major European systems, besides British Railways, to be considered in detail. Reasons for this, apart from the dictates of space, are first that the SNCF is the largest; second, since World War II it has been the most progressive and an example of what can be achieved with strong government commitment, unlike British Railways on which progress has been hampered by low investment and apathetic government. Third, information about the SNCF has been forthcoming.

On the world's largest nationalised system, the USSR Railways, scant information is available compared with the railways of Britain, France, USA, Canada, Australia and Japan, on which there is an abundance of factual material. It has not been practicable to present information in a standard form because different railway managements tend to stress different aspects of their statistics, but as far as possible the aim has been to enable comparisons to be made between various railways and to present an outline of the progress or decline within a system over a number of years.

Certain railways cannot be compared; for example the railways of Europe and of the USA. In the USA the most economical method of operating freight traffic over the enormous distances is to assemble it into trains up to 2 km (1.25 miles) long, often hauled by six or more diesel locomotives, under the control of two or three men. Such trains would be unmanageable in Europe where distances are much shorter and traffic density much greater, and where track layouts could not accommodate such trains.

A similar rule applies to electrification: it is an economic proposition only if the traffic density is such as to make the installation cost worthwhile. Eventually, however, rising fuel costs may make electric railways the most economical form of transport even in the USA. In the USSR, where greater distances are involved, rail traffic density is sufficient to justify electrification on a vast scale, such as on the Trans-Siberian Railway. An interesting feature of the USSR Railways is that the equipment is almost identical with that in North America.

Unfortunately, it is not yet possible to give full details of the railway system on which the greatest progress is being made, The Chinese People's Republic Railways; but gradually, as the significance of the work they are doing is realised, details are emerging and soon it should be possible to give much more information about the railways of this fascinating country which aims to have 60 000 km (nearly 40 000 miles) of railway route by 1990.

A book of this type is out of date before it is even typed; by the time it is published, route lengths, numbers of locomotives and rolling stock, all have changed. The numbers quoted were from the most recent information, but at best can be only approximate.

Although most of the information in this book is obtainable in various printed sources, some of which are not readily available, it is believed that this is the only book in which the information from these numerous sources is brought together in one compact volume.

Throughout the book metric units are given first, followed by imperial units in brackets. For countries using the metric system, the metric units are the original measurements, the imperial the conversion, and vice versa.

# 1 Important Dates in Railway History

**1758** Middleton Railway, Leeds, authorised on 9 June by Britain's first Railway Act which described it as a 'wagonway'.

**1801** Surrey Iron Railway incorporated on 21 May; the first public railway to be sanctioned by Parliament. Opened from Wandsworth to Croydon on 26 July 1803 and extended by the Croydon, Merstham & Godstone Railway, incorporated on 17 May 1803 and opened from Croydon to Merstham on 24 July 1805.

**1804** On 22 February a steam locomotive by Richard Trevithick, his second, hauled a load of 10 tons of iron, 70 men and five extra wagons for 15 km (9½ miles) at nearly 8 km/h (5 mph) at Penydarren Ironworks near Merthyr Tydfil in South Wales. It ran on 'L' section rails.

Oystermouth Railway, or Tramroad, Company incorporated on 29 June to build a railway from Swansea to Mumbles in South Wales. It was opened about 1806, and on 25 March 1807 became the first railway in the world to convey fare-paying passengers. It was closed on 5 January 1960.

**1808** Kilmarnock & Troon Railway incorporated on 27 May, the first 'proper' railway in Scotland. It opened on 6 July 1812 and was operated by horses until steam traction was introduced in 1817.

**1812** Steam traction introduced, 12 August, on the Middleton Railway, Leeds (see 9 June 1758), using a system of toothed wheel and rack propulsion patented by John Blenkinsop (qv).

**1814** George Stephenson's first steam locomotive, named *Blücher*, completed at Killingworth near Newcastle-upon-Tyne, on 25 July.

**1823** Concession granted on 26 February for the St Etienne–Andrézieux Railway, the first in France. (See 1 October 1828)

**1825** Stockton & Darlington Railway opened on 27 September, when George Stephenson's locomotive *Locomotion* hauled a long train of passengers and coal.

**1826** Liverpool & Manchester Railway incorporated on 5 May. (See 15 September 1830)

**1827** Baltimore & Ohio Railroad incorporated on 28 February. (See 24 May 1830)

The first railway in the Austrian Empire opened on 7 September from Budweis (Ceske Budejovice) to Trojanov, part of the Linz–Budweis Railway. Horse traction was used.

**1828** Bolton & Leigh Railway, Lancashire, opened on 1 August, using steam power.

First railway in France opened on 1 October from St Etienne to Andrézieux with horse traction. It was unofficially brought into use in May 1827. Passenger traffic began on 1 March 1832. Steam traction was introduced in 1844.

**1829** Rainhill Trials on the Liverpool & Manchester Railway, 6–14 October, when the steam locomotive established itself as a reliable form of motive power.

**1830** Canterbury & Whitstable Railway opened on 3 May, also using steam power.

First section of the Baltimore & Ohio Railroad opened on 24 May between Baltimore and Ellicott's Mills, Maryland.

Liverpool & Manchester Railway opened on 15 September, the first 'modern' main-line railway.

**1834** Wigan Branch and Wigan & Preston Railways amalgamated by the first railway amalgamation Act on 22 May to form the North Union Railway, in Lancashire.

First railway in Ireland opened on 17 December between Dublin and Kingstown (later Dun Laoghaire). It was built to standard gauge, but was rebuilt to the Irish gauge of 1600 mm (5 ft 3 in) in 1857.

**1835** On 7 December the first railway in Germany, the Ludwigsbahn between Nuremberg and Fürth, opened with Stephenson's locomotive *Der Adler*.

**1836** First railway in London opened on 8 February, from Spa Road to Deptford, part of the London & Greenwich Railway. Extended to London Bridge 14 December 1836 and to Greenwich 24 December 1838.

Festiniog Railway in Wales opened on 20 April for slate traffic. With a gauge of 600 mm (1 ft 11½ in) it was the world's first narrow-gauge railway. Steam traction, the first on a narrow gauge, began in 1863.

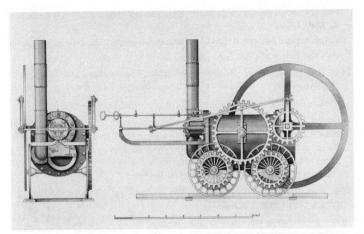

Trevithick's Coalbrookdale locomotive, 1803. Drawing by the Science Museum, London. It was probably intended for the tramway at Coalbrookdale Ironworks, Shropshire, but there is no evidence that it actually ran. (The Science Museum, London)

Passenger traffic, official as distinct from 'rides', began on 6 January 1865.

First steam railway in Canada, the Champlain & St Lawrence, opened on 21 July between Laprairie and St John. The first locomotive was *Dorchester* by Robert Stephenson & Co.

First railway in Russia opened on 9 October, with horse traction, from Pavlosk to Tsarskoe Selo, as part of the St Petersburg & Pavlovsk Railway, built to a gauge of 1829 mm (6 ft). The first locomotive was built by Robert Stephenson & Co in 1836.

**1837** Grand Junction Railway opened on 4 July between Birmingham and Warrington, the first British trunk railway, or main line connecting the London & Birmingham with the Liverpool & Manchester. By 1848 it had become part of the main line from London to Glasgow.

**1838** First railway wholly in modern Austria, the Kaiser Ferdinand Nordbahn, opened on 6 January from Vienna to Floridsdorf and Deutsch Wagram.

First section of the Great Western Railway opened on 4 June from London (Paddington) to Maidenhead, to Brunel's 2134 mm (7 ft) gauge. It

11

was opened to Bristol on 30 June 1841. The last broad-gauge trains ran on 20 May 1892.

London & Birmingham Railway opened throughout on 17 September. It was the first main line into London.

**1839** First railway in the Netherlands, Amsterdam to Haarlem, opened on 24 September.

First railway in Italy, Naples to Portici, opened on 4 October.

On 14 November the first royal railway journey was made by Prince Albert and his brother Ernest from Slough to London Paddington. Queen Victoria first travelled by train, also from Slough to Paddington, on 13 June 1842. The first reigning monarch to travel by train was Frederick William IV of Prussia, on 24 January 1842.

**1841** Manchester & Leeds Railway, the first railway to cross the Pennine range, opened on 1 March.

**1842** Edinburgh & Glasgow Railway opened on 21 February.

**1844** First railway in Switzerland, Basel to St Ludwig (St Louis, France), opened on 15 June. (See 9 June 1847)

**1846** First railway in Hungary, Pest to Vacz, opened on 15 July.

Gauge Act given Royal Assent on 18 August. By making a 'loop hole' it failed in its intention to standardise the gauge of railways in Britain.

'Railway Mania' in Britain; 273 railway bills received the Royal Assent during the year.

**1847** First railway in modern Denmark opened on 26 June, from Copenhagen to Roskilde. The Altona–Kiel Railway, opened in 1844, was in territory later annexed by Prussia.

Zurich–Baden Railway opened on 9 August, the first railway wholly in Switzerland.

**1848** On 15 February the Caledonian Railway was opened from Carlisle to Edinburgh and Glasgow, completing the 'West Coast Route' (so called because it skirts the west coast for about 400 yards in the course of its 400 miles from London to Glasgow). (See 1 April 1850)

First railway in Spain, Barcelona to Mataro, opened on 28 October.

First railway in South America, Georgetown to Plaisance, British Guyana, opened on 3 November. It was closed on 30 June 1972.

**1850** On 1 April the British 'West Coast Route' was completed to Perth and Aberdeen (on the east coast) by the Scottish North Eastern Railway.

The 'East Coast Route' from London to Edinburgh and Glasgow was completed on 7 August with the opening of the Great Northern Railway from Werrington Junction, Peterborough, to London (Maiden Lane). Trains used a temporary bridge over the Tweed into Berwick until the Royal Border Bridge came into use on 29 August 1850. The 'Towns Line', Werrington Junction–Grantham–Newark–Retford, was opened on 1 August 1852, and the extension from Maiden Lane to Kings Cross on 14 October 1852.

**1851** On 1 November train services began on the Moscow–St Petersburg Railway (Nikolaev Railway).

**1853** First railway in India, Bombay to Thana, opened on 18 April by the Great Indian Peninsula Railway Company.

**1854** First railway in Brazil opened on 30 April, from Maua at the end of the Bay of Rio to the foot of the Petropolis Serra. It was built to a gauge of 1676 mm (5 ft 6 in) and later converted to metre gauge.

First public railway in Australia to carry passengers and goods, the Port Elliot & Goolwa Railway in South Australia, opened on 18 May using horse traction.

First railway in Norway, Oslo (then Christiania) to Eidsvoll, opened on 1 September.

On 12 September the first steam-operated railway in Australia was opened, from Melbourne (Flinders Street) to Port Melbourne, Victoria. It is now part of the Victoria Government system.

**1855** World's first special postal train inaugurated on 1 February by the GWR between London and Bristol. Passengers were carried from June 1869 when a first-class carriage was attached.

First railway in New South Wales, Australia, opened from Sydney to Parramatta on 26 September.

**1856** In January train services began on the first railway in Africa, Alexandria to Cairo, 210 km (130 miles).

Through trains began running on 27 October between Montreal and Toronto on the Grand Trunk Railway.

First railway in Portugal, Lisbon to Carregado, opened on 28 October.

First sections of Swedish State Railways opened, Gothenburg to Jonsered and Malmö to Lund, brought into use on 1 December.

Interlocking of signals and points patented by John Saxby (qv).

**1857** On 30 August the first railway in Argentina was opened, Parque to

A Blenkinsop locomotive on the Middleton Railway, Leeds, built by Matthew Murray, 1812. (The Science Museum, London)

Swansea & Mumbles electric railway, South Wales. On 25 March 1807, about a year after opening, it became the first railway in the world to carry fare-paying passengers. It was electrified in 1929, and closed on 5 January 1960. Photographed at Mumbles in the last summer of operation, on 27 August 1959. (John Marshall)

Reproduction *Sans Pareil* and Liverpool & Manchester Railway coach, followed by 0–4–2 *Lion* near St Helens Junction, Lancashire, on 25 May 1980, during the celebration of the 150th anniversary of the opening. (John Marshall)

Curzon Street Station, Birmingham, terminus of the London & Birmingham Railway from 9 April 1838 when it was opened from Birmingham to Rugby. Closed to passengers on 1 July 1854 when New Street Station was opened. (John Marshall)

Floresta, to the Indian standard gauge of 1676 mm (5 ft 6 in) because the first locomotive, *La Portenta* of 1856, was built by E. B. Wilson & Co of Leeds for an Indian railway of that gauge.

**1860** First railway in South Africa, Durban to the Point (Natal), opened on 26 June by the Natal Railway Co Ltd. It was acquired by the Natal Government on 1 January 1877.

**1861** First railway in what is now Pakistan, from Karachi City to Kotri, opened on 13 May.

**1863** First city underground railway, the Metropolitan Railway, London, from Bishop's Road to Farringdon Street, on 10 January.

First steam-operated railway in New Zealand, Christchurch to Ferrymead, opened on 1 December with a gauge of 1600 mm (5 ft 3 in). It was later converted to 1067 mm (3 ft 6 in) gauge, standard in New Zealand.

**1865** First railway in Sri Lanka (Ceylon), from Colombo to Ambepussa, 2 October.

**1869** Completion on 10 May of the first North American trans-continental railway at Promontory, north of the Great Salt Lake, Utah, USA, by the joining of the Union Pacific and Central Pacific Railroads.

First railway in Roumania opened on 19 October, from Bucharest to Giurgiu.

**1872** First railway in Japan opened on 12 June from Yokohama to Shinagawa. It was completed to Tokyo (then Yedo or Jeddo) on 14 October 1872.

**1878** First Tay Bridge, designed by Thomas Bouch, brought into use on 1 June. The middle spans blew down in a gale while a train was crossing on 28 December 1879. The present Tay Bridge designed by W. H. Barlow was opened on 20 June 1887. It remains the longest railway bridge in Europe, 3552 m (11 653 ft).

**1879** From 31 May to 30 September Werner von Siemens operated the first practical electric railway at the Berlin Trades Exhibition. The 3hp locomotive pulled 30 passengers at 6.5 km/h (4 mph).

**1880** First permanent railway in China.

**1881** First public electric railway in the world opened near Lichterfelde near Berlin on 12 May. It was 2.5 km (1½ miles) long. The car ran on a 100 V supply and carried 26 passengers at 48 km/h (30 mph).

**1883** Magnus Volk's Electric Railway opened on 4 August at Brighton;

Britain's first electric railway. It was taken over by Brighton Corporation on 1 April 1940 and still operates each summer.

**1884** London's Inner Circle (Metropolitan and District Railways) and the connection with the East London Railway through Marc Brunel's Thames Tunnel completed on 6 October.

**1885** Canada's first trans-continental railway, the Canadian Pacific, completed in British Columbia on 7 November. The first train across Canada left Montreal on 28 June 1886 and arrived at Port Moody on 4 July. The 19.3 km (12 miles) extension to Vancouver was opened on 23 May 1887, completing a main line of 4635 km (2879 miles).

**1889** Regulation of Railways Act, enforcing the block system, interlocking of signals and points, and provision of automatic continuous brakes on British passenger trains, received the Royal Assent on 30 August.

**1890** Forth Bridge, near Edinburgh, opened by King Edward VII on 4 March. It remains the world's largest railway cantilever bridge.

City & South London Railway opened on 8 December, the first electric underground railway.

**1893** On 6 March the first section of the Liverpool Overhead Railway was brought into use, the first electric elevated city railway in the world. It was closed on 31 December 1956.

**1901** Trans-Siberian Railway opened on 3 November to Vladivostock, the world's longest railway, using a ferry across Lake Baikal. The Circum-Baikal line was completed on 25 September 1904. The distance from Moscow to Vladivostock is 9336 km (5801 miles).

**1903** On 3 May electrification was completed on the Mersey Railway, the first steam railway in Britain to be converted to electric operation.

**1904** First section of Tyneside electrification brought into use by the North Eastern Railway on 29 March, the first British suburban railway electrification. It was closely followed by the Lancashire & Yorkshire Railway Liverpool to Southport line, brought partly into use on 5 April 1904.

**1905** London 'Inner Circle' electrification inaugurated on 12 April. The last steam trains were withdrawn on 22 September 1905.

**1906** Simplon tunnel (Switzerland–Italy), 19 803 m (12 miles 537 yd) long, first used on 25 January. It was opened 1 June 1906.

**1910** Trans-Andine Railway opened between Los Andes, Chile, and Mendosa, Argentina, on 5 April. It is metre gauge.

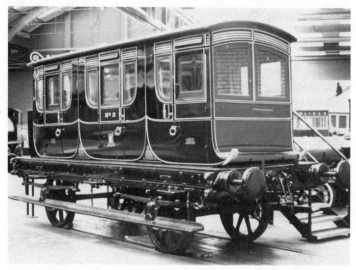

Queen Adelaide's coach, 1842, the first royal railway carriage, preserved in the National Railway Museum, York. It measures 6.64 m (21 ft 9 in) over buffers and stands 3 m (9 ft 10 in) high. The body is only 1.68 m (5 ft 6 in) wide. The vehicle has no brakes. (John Marshall)

**1915** Britain's worst railway disaster occurred on 22 May, when 224 lives were lost in the double collision at Quintinshill north of Carlisle, a result of signalling irregularities.

**1917** Trans-Australian Railway opened on 22 October by Commonwealth Railways. In its 1693 km (1052 miles) between Kalgoorlie and Port Augusta it traverses the Nullarbor Plain for 478 km (297 miles) without a curve, the world's longest straight stretch of railway.

**1921** Railways Act, ruling that most of Britain's railway companies should be amalgamated into four groups for greater efficiency and economy of operation, received the Royal Assent on 19 August.

**1923** On 1 January 123 separate British railway companies amalgamated into four groups; the London, Midland & Scottish; London & North Eastern; Great Western; and Southern.

**1928** The world's longest non-stop run, between London and Edinburgh, 632.5 km (393 miles), inaugurated by the LNER on 1 May.

**1931** Airscrew-driven railcar reaches a world record rail speed of 230 km/h (143 mph) for 10 km (6¼ miles) between Karstadt and Dergenthin, Germany, on 21 June.

**1938** On 3 July LNER 4-6-2 No 4468 *Mallard* achieved the world speed record for steam traction of 201 km/h (125 mph) between Grantham, Lincolnshire, and Peterborough, Cambridgeshire.

**1947** Transport Act received Royal Assent on 6 August, providing for nationalisation of British rail, road and canal transport.

**1948** Nationalisation of British railways on 1 January.

**1952** Double collision at Harrow on 8 October when 112 were killed in the worst passenger train accident in England. It accelerated the programme for equipping all main lines with the Automatic Warning System.

**1954** Britain's first 'all electric' main line, between Manchester and Sheffield, fully opened for passenger and goods trains on 14 September, using the 1500 V dc overhead system. The passenger service was withdrawn on 5 January 1970 and transferred to the Midland route to make space for freight traffic, despite the line's increased capacity. The

A railway viaduct which never carried trains. Duddeston Viaduct in Birmingham which the Great Western Railway was forced to build in 1852 to connect with the LNWR, under its Act of 1846, but which was never used. Photographed on 14 June 1984. (John Marshall)

freight traffic was withdrawn from 18 July 1981 and the line abandoned between Hadfield and Penistone, including the new Woodhead tunnel.

**1955** On 28 March a French 1500 V dc electric train reached a world record speed of 230.9 km/h (205.6 mph) for 2 km (1.24 miles) with 4300 hp Co-Co locomotive No 7107.

Car Sleeper service introduced on 15 June by British Railways between London and Perth. Private motor cars were carried on flat wagons behind sleeping cars.

**1956** British Railways decided on 6 March to adopt 25 kV 50 Hz system as the standard for future electrification.

**1959** First section of British 25 kV electric railway brought into operation on 16 March on the Colchester–Clacton–Walton line, 39.5 km (24½ miles). The first main-line installation, between Crewe and Manchester, came into operation on 12 September 1960.

At Swindon, in March, the last steam locomotive was completed for British Railways, 2-10-0 No 92220 *Evening Star*.

**1960** On 25 April Steam locomotives were finally withdrawn from Canadian National Railways. In 1950 there were about 2500 steam locomotives.

**1964** New standard-gauge Shinkansen line opened on 1 October between Osaka and Tokyo.

**1965** Japan introduced the first regular scheduled service at over 161 km/h (100 mph) on the Shinkansen line on 1 November.

**1968** Steam traction eliminated from British Railways, on 8 August, except on the narrow-gauge Vale of Rheidol Line in Wales.

**1970** Chengtu–Kunming railway, China, opened on 1 July. In its 1085 km/ (674 miles) it has 427 tunnels and 653 bridges. The combined length of tunnels and bridges exceeds 400 km, about 250 miles.

**1973** Highest speed with diesel traction, 232 km/h (143 mph) reached on 12 June by British Railways high-speed diesel train between Northallerton and Thirsk on the Darlington–York section.

**1975** First electrified trunk railway in China opened on 1 July between Chengtu and Paochi, 676 km (420 miles), in the Province of Szechwan, on the 25 kV 50 Hz system.

On 10 August gas turbine powered experimental Advanced Passenger Train (APT-E) maintained a speed of 244.6 km/h (152 mph) for 8 km (5 miles) between Swindon and Reading.

**1976** BR introduces High Speed Trains (HSTs) between London (Paddington) and Bristol and South Wales on 4 October.

**1978** New Merseyrail system completely opened on 3 January.

On 8 May BR introduced HSTs between London (Kings Cross) and Edinburgh, covering 632 km (392.7 miles) in 4 h 52 min.

**1979** First section, 835 km (519 miles), of the railway in Lhasa in Tibet opened on 1 October by the Chinese People Republic Railways.

On 20 December BR electric Advanced Passenger Train on test reached a speed of 257.5 km (160 mph) in Dumfriesshire, Scotland.

**1980** First section of Tyne & Wear Metro, Haymarket to Tynemouth, opened to passengers on 1 August. The final section, to South Shields, was opened on 24 March 1984.

**1981** On French Railways on 27 September TGV (Train à Grande Vitesse) trains began a regular hourly service between Paris and Lyon, 426 km (265 miles) in 2 h 40 min.

# 2 Railway Makers

**ADAMS, William Bridges**, 1797–1872. British Inventor of the railcar (1843), rail fishplate (1847) and radial axlebox (1863).

**ALLCARD, William**, 1809–61. British Locomotive engineer and railway contractor on various early railway projects including Lancaster & Preston Junction Railway. From 1841 to 61 worked with Buddicom, Locke and Mackenzie (qqv) on the Paris–Rouen and other French railways.

**ALLEN, Horatio**, 1802–90. American locomotive pioneer and civil engineer. Visited England in 1826 to study railway construction and to order material for the Delaware & Hudson Railroad, including a locomotive, *Stourbridge Lion*, which he drove at the opening of the railroad in 1829.

**ARMSTRONG, George**, 1822–1901. Locomotive engineer on the Great Western Railway, England. Locomotive superintendent of the Northern Division at Wolverhampton 1864–97.

**ARROL, Sir William**, 1839–1913. Civil engineering contractor and bridge builder. His greatest works were the second Tay Bridge at Dundee (1887), the Forth Bridge near Edinburgh (1890) when he was knighted by Queen Victoria, and the Queen Alexandra Bridge at Sunderland (1909).

**ASPINALL, Sir John**, 1851–1937. Chief mechanical engineer (1886–99) and general manager (1899–1919) of the Lancashire & Yorkshire Railway, England. He completed the locomotive works at Horwich near Bolton, making it one of the most modern in the world at that time (1886–9). He was a pioneer in the adoption of a system of standard components which could be used in a variety of locomotive designs. Also he was a pioneer of railway electrification, on the Liverpool–Southport line in 1904. In 1916 he electrified the Manchester–Bury line.

**BAKER, Sir Benjamin**, 1840–1907. Civil engineer, famous for his design for the Forth Bridge (1883–90). With John Fowler and J. H. Greathead (qqv) Baker was concerned with the first London tube railways (1890-1900).

**BALDWIN, Matthias William**, 1795–1866. Locomotive engineer and manufacturer and founder of the largest locomotive works in the USA, near Philadelphia. He built his first locomotive in 1832. At the time of his death his firm had built 1500 locomotives. In 1955 it produced its last steam locomotive, having produced about 75 000.

**BARLOW, William Henry,** 1812–1902. Chief civil engineer on the Midland Railway, England, from its formation in 1844 until succeeded by Crossley in 1858. In 1862–9 he engineered the Midland Railway extension from Bedford to St Pancras, London, including the great roof at St Pancras station, 30.5 m (100 ft) high with a span of 73 m (240 ft). In 1860 he and Hawkshaw (qv) completed Brunel's Clifton suspension bridge at Bristol.

**BASSETT-LOWKE, Wenman Joseph,** 1877–1953. Born in Northampton, England. Designer and builder of model steam locomotives and ships. In collaboration with Henry Greenly (1876–1947) he built locomotives for several 381 mm (15 in) gauge railways.

**BEATTIE, Joseph Hamilton,** 1808–71. Locomotive superintendent on the London & South Western Railway from 1850 until his death. He took out many patents for improvements in locomotives, including a feed-water heater and a firebox for burning coal.

**BELPAIRE, Alfred Jules,** 1820–93. Belgian locomotive engineer and designer of the firebox (1860–4) named after him and still in use on numerous steam locomotives around the world.

**BETTS, Edward Ladds,** 1815–72. Railway contractor. As early as age 18 he was responsible under Locke (qv) for construction of the Dutton Viaduct on the Grand Junction Railway, England. In partnership with Peto and Brassey (qqv) he carried out numerous railway contracts in Britain and abroad, including the Grand Trunk Railway, Canada, with the bridge over the St Lawrence at Montreal.

**BEYER, Charles Frederick,** 1813–76. Locomotive engineer and manufacturer, born in Saxony. Settled in Manchester, England, where he designed locomotives for Sharp, Roberts & Co. In 1854 he joined Richard Peacock (qv) to found the famous locomotive building firm of Beyer Peacock in Manchester, builders of locomotives for railways throughout the world.

**BIDDER, George Parker,** 1806–78. Civil engineer and notable mathematician. Worked on the laying out of many early British railways; also advised on the laying out of the Belgian railway system and a large portion of the Great Eastern Railway in England. With Robert Stephenson (qv) he built the first railway in Norway, Christiania (Oslo) to Eidsvoll. As consulting engineer for Indian railways he was responsible for the establishment of the 1.676 m (5 ft 6 in) gauge.

**BLENKINSOP, John,** 1783–1831. British Steam locomotive pioneer who, in conjunction with Matthew Murray (qv) in 1811 patented a toothed wheel and rack system for propelling steam locomotives. Four such locomotives were built by Murray from 1812 and they worked on the Middleton Colliery Railway near Leeds for 20 years. They were the first commercially successful steam locomotives.

**BRADSHAW, George,** 1801–53. Printer in Manchester, England. His connection with railways began with his maps. His first railway timetable appeared in 1839. His *General Railway Directory and Shareholder's Guide* appeared annually from 1849 to 1923. The last Bradshaw timetable, No 1521, was published in June 1961.

**BRASSEY, Thomas,** 1805–70. British Civil engineer and railway contractor. His first railway contract, under Locke (qv), was for part of the Grand Junction Railway in 1835. Besides many miles of railway in Great Britain his firm, singly or in partnership with Mackenzie, Peto and Betts, undertook numerous contracts all over the world. In 1843–8 he was employing about 75 000 men. His railway contracts 1848–61 amounted to 3871 km (2374 miles) at a cost of £28 million.

**BRUNEL, Isambard Kingdom,** 1806–59. Civil engineer. Began his training under his father, Sir Marc Isambard Brunel (1769–1849) in the Thames Tunnel, London, completed in 1842. In 1833 he was appointed engineer of the Great Western Railway and he laid out the line from London to Bristol with a gauge of 7 ft (2.134 m). It was opened in 1841. It included the Box Tunnel 2937 m (1 mile 1452 yd). He engineered the continuation of the railway to Exeter, Plymouth and over his great Saltash Bridge to Penzance, and from Swindon to Gloucester and South Wales, with another large bridge at Chepstow. He also achieved fame as a designer and builder of steamships. His greatest ship, *Great Eastern*, begun in 1853, produced so many anxieties that it contributed to his early death at the age of only 53.

**BRUNLEES, Sir James,** 1816–92. Civil engineer on railways in Great Britain and abroad. His first railway work was with Alexander Adie (1808–79) on the Bolton & Preston Railway. Later he worked with Locke and Errington (qqv) on railways in Scotland. His greatest achievement was the laying out of the São Paulo Railway in Brazil (1851) up the famous cable-worked inclines through trackless jungle. With Charles Douglas Fox (1840–1921) he engineered the Mersey Railway with a 3493 m (3820 yd) tunnel under the river. In conjunction with John Hawkshaw (qv) he was engineer to the original Channel Tunnel project.

**BUDDICOM, William Barber,** 1816–87. Locomotive and civil engineer and contractor. After experience on the Liverpool & Manchester Railway he became, at the age of 24, locomotive superintendent of the Grand Junction Railway at the same time as the transfer of the GJR locomotive works from Edge Hill, Liverpool, to Crewe. Frequent breakages of crank axles on the Stephenson 'Patentee' type engines led Buddicom to introduce the 'Crewe' type engine with outside cylinders supported in outside framing. Buddicom later developed the design in France, and it was also used on the Caledonian and Highland Railways. An example is preserved in the National Railway Museum at York. In 1841 he left the GJR to work under Locke (qv) in France designing and building locomotives for the Paris & Rouen Railway and other French railways, and with Brassey (qv) on the construction of various railways in France.

**BULLEID, Oliver Vaughan Snell,** 1882–1970. British Locomotive engineer. He was trained under H. A. Ivatt (qv) on the Great Northern Railway at Doncaster and from 1912 he worked there as assistant to H. N. Gresley (qv). In 1937 he was appointed chief mechanical engineer of the Southern Railway on which he introduced revolutionary designs of 0–6–0 and 4–6–2 locomotives. His last design for the SR, the 'Leader' class, was an expensive failure. In 1949 he became CME on the Irish Railways at Dublin where he designed and built a turf-burning locomotive.

**BURY, Edward,** 1794–1858. Before 1829 he had established a works in Liverpool for the design and manufacture of locomotives. He established the bar-frame construction which became standard in North American locomotive practice. Most of his designs were small four-wheeled types with fireboxes of 'D' pattern (in plan). He was responsible for the locomotive department of the London & Birmingham Railway 1838–46 and of the Great Northern Railway 1847–50, while continuing his building practice at Liverpool. It was the under-pricing of a batch of plate-framed 2–2–2s for the Lancashire & Yorkshire Railway which brought about closure of the firm in 1850 after building 415 locomotives. A typical Bury locomotive, Furness Railway 'Coppernob', is preserved in the National Railway Museum at York.

**CAPROTTI, Arturo,** 1881–1938. Italian locomotive engineer and inventor of the poppet valve gear (1916), based on petrol engine practice, which bears his name. It was first used in Italy in 1920 and in Britain in 1926. It resulted in considerable coal economies in engines with poor front-end design, but it was expensive to maintain and had no advantage over well designed long-travel long-lap valve gear.

**CHAPELON, Andre,** 1892–1978. French locomotive engineer who developed the steam locomotive to the most advanced state of efficiency yet achieved. In conjunction with the Finnish engineer Kylälä he designed a

25

new exhaust system which was named the Kylchap (1926) and which greatly improved locomotive performance by producing a good draught with minimum back pressure. He redesigned and enlarged steam passages to reduce throttling losses. His greatest locomotive, and perhaps the greatest steam locomotive of all time, was his three-cylinder compound 4–8–4 242A1, rebuilt from a three-cylinder simple 4–8–2 in 1942–6. His principles influenced Gresley (qv) and engineers in Argentina and Brazil.

CHURCHWARD, George Jackson, 1857–1933. Locomotive engineer on the Great Western Railway, England. After three years on the South Devon Railway he was transferred to Swindon in 1876 under Joseph Armstrong (1816–77, brother of George, qv) and later William Dean (1840–1905). In 1897 he became chief assistant to Dean who gave him freedom to experiment with Belpaire boilers and even a new design of 4–6–0 (1902), the forerunner of the 'Saints', 'Halls' and 'Granges'. That year he became chief mechanical engineer and he proceeded to equip the GWR with a stud of fine locomotives using a range of standard components such as boilers, cylinders and wheels. In his adoption of superheating and long-travel piston valves he was years ahead of his contemporary British engineers.

COOK, Thomas, 1808–92. Founder of the famous British firm of travel agents. Began by arranging some of the first railway excursions, from Leicester, in 1841. He developed the business until he was organising tours all over the world.

CRAMPTON, Thomas Russell, 1816–88. British civil and locomotive engineer. In 1842, while working with Daniel Gooch (qv) on the Great Western Railway, he designed his famous 'single-driver' type locomotive with the driving axle behind the firebox which made possible a large low-pitched boiler, and he took out a patent in 1843. He left the GWR in 1844. The first two Crampton engines were built for Belgium in 1845. Others followed for the LNWR and for the Dundee & Perth Railway in 1848. The greatest British example was the LNWR 6–2–0 Liverpool in 1848. A total of 320 'Cramptons' were built, mostly in France (where one is preserved), Germany and Belgium.

DE GLEHN, Alfred George, 1848–1936. French locomotive engineer, and pioneer of steam locomotive compounding. His first four-cylinder compound was built for the Northern Railway of France in 1866. The two high-pressure cylinders outside drove the rear driving wheels and the two low-pressure cylinders inside drove the forward axle. The famous Nord 'Atlantics' appeared in 1890 and so impressed Churchward (qv) on the GWR in England that he ordered one in 1903 and two more in 1905.

The largest De Glehn compounds were the 1.676 m (5 ft 6 in) gauge 4–6–2s built for India in 1928. On the standard gauge its development was restricted by the limitations on the size of the inside low-pressure cylinders.

**DIESEL, Dr Rudolph,** 1858–1913. German engineer. Famous for the design of the compression-ignition oil engine named after him, but which was first invented in 1890 by Herbert Akroyd Stuart (1864–1927). The diesel engine was developed by Maschinenfabrik Augsburg, Nürnberg (MAN) from 1893. Its first application to rail traction was in a Sulzer-Diesel locomotive completed at Winterthur, Switzerland, in 1913 for the Prusso-Hessian State Railway, Berlin.

**DÜBS, Henry,** 1816–76. Trained in Germany as a mechanical engineer. Visited England in 1839 to see engineering works and settled there, becoming works manager at Vulcan Foundry, Lancashire, in 1842. In 1858 he went to Glasgow and with W. M. Neilson (1819–89) laid out the Hyde Park Locomotive Works at Springburn. In 1865 he opened up his own works in Glasgow. Dübs & Co became part of the North British Locomotive Co in 1903.

**EDMONDSON, Thomas,** 1792–1851. Born at Lancaster, England. Originator of the standard card railway tickets, of a machine for printing them (1837) and a press for stamping dates on the tickets. Almost identical date presses and other equipment of his invention are still in use today.

**EIFFEL, Alexandre Gustav,** 1832–1923. French civil engineer, best known for his Paris tower of 1887–9 but also designer of many large iron bridges and viaducts: Tagus Bridge in Spain (1880), Garabit Viaduct, France, (1882), Tardes Viaduct, Central France, (1883) and others. By 1887 the iron and steelwork in his railway bridges totalled 38 000 tons.

**ERRINGTON, John Edward,** 1806–62. Civil engineer, associated with Locke (qv) whom he met while resident engineer on the Grand Junction Railway, England. His principal work was jointly with Locke as engineers of the Lancaster & Carlisle; and the Caledonian and other railways in Scotland.

**FAIRBAIRN, Sir William,** 1789–1874. Engineer in Manchester, England; builder of locomotives and designer and builder of bridges. He was born in Roxburghshire, Scotland, but settled in Manchester in 1813. Started his engineering works in 1817. Locomotive building began in 1839, mostly Bury (qv) designs, and he built about 400. In conjunction with Robert Stephenson (qv) he designed and tested the tubular girder used on the Conway and Menai Strait bridges on the Chester & Holyhead Railway.

**FALSHAW, Sir James,** 1810–89. Civil engineer and contractor. The first railway construction project of which he was put in charge was the Lancaster & Carlisle (1844). Most of his work was on main lines in Scotland.

**FOWLER, Sir John,** 1817–98. Civil engineer, best known as engineer of the Metropolitan Railway in London, Responsible for 18 km (11 miles) out of the 21 km (13 miles) of the 'Inner Circle' (1860–3). In partnership with Baker (qv) he shared in the construction of the Forth Bridge (1883–90).

**FOX, Sir (Charles) Douglas,** 1840–1921. British Civil engineer and contractor, son of Sir Charles Fox (1810–74), also a noted railway engineer. Worked with his father 1860–74 on various railway bridge projects including Battersea, London.

**GARRATT, Herbert William,** 1864–1913. Inventor of the 'Garratt' articulated steam locomotive, an engine unit at each end connected by a frame carrying the boiler, which he patented in 1907. The design was taken up by Beyer Peacock & Co of Manchester, England, who built the first two, for Tasmania, in 1909. One of these is now preserved in the National Railway Museum at York. Garratts were built for railways throughout the world. The last Garratts were 610 mm (2 ft) gauge machines built for South Africa in 1968.

**GIFFARD, Henri,** 1825–82. French balloonist, best known in railway circles for his invention of the steam injector in 1859. This made it possible to inject water into the boiler while the locomotive was stationary, but axle-driven pumps continued in use for many years afterwards.

**GÖLSDORF, Dr Karl,** 1861–1916. Austrian locomotive engineer. Became chief mechanical engineer of Austrian State Railways in 1891. Designed about 60 classes of capable locomotives for the varied and extremely difficult routes of Austria which then included large areas now in Italy.

**GOOCH, Sir Daniel,** 1816–89. First locomotive superintendent and later chairman of the Great Western Railway, England. After experience on various railways he was appointed to the GWR in 1837 at the age of 21. It was Gooch who established the GWR locomotive works at Swindon in 1840, building the first locomotive there in 1846. He resigned in 1864, to be succeeded by Joseph Armstrong (1816–77), and he worked on Brunel's great iron ship *Great Eastern* to lay the first trans-Atlantic cable, completed in 1866, for which he was made a baronet. In 1865 he was asked to become chairman of the GWR, whose affairs were then in a low state, and in this position he guided the company to success. He saw the Severn Tunnel through to completion in 1887.

London & North Western Railway Buddicom 'Crewe' type 2–2–2 of 1845 at the National Railway Museum, York, 1 August 1983. (John Marshall)

The largest French express passenger engine, 3-cylinder compound 4–8–4 No 242–A–1, rebuilt by Chapelon in 1946. (SNCF/French Railways Ltd)

The last locomotive design by George Jackson Churchward on the Great Western Railway, 2–8–0 No 4704 on a Bristol to London freight train at Swindon on 8 April 1960. (John Marshall)

'Fairlie Centenary' special at Tan-y-Grisiau, Festiniog Railway, 13 October 1979, headed by *Merddin Emrys* built in 1879 (leading) and *Earl of Merioneth* built in 1979. (John Marshall)

Train at Dymchurch on the 381 mm (15 in) gauge Romney, Hythe & Dymchurch Railway, headed by 4–6–2 No 2 *Northern Chief*, 21 August 1973. (John Marshall)

*River Esk* on a train entering Ravenglass on the 381 mm (15 in) gauge Ravenglass & Eskdale Railway, 28 June 1976. (John Marshall)

Gölsdorf 2−6−4 No 301.05 at Vienna Railway Museum, 30 July 1975. The design dates from 1911. Driving wheels are 2100 mm (6 ft 10⅝ in) diameter. (John Marshall)

London & North Eastern Railway 2−8−2 No 2001 *Cock o' the North*, designed by H. N. Gresley and built at Doncaster in 1934. Shown as originally built with Lentz rotary cam poppet valve gear. Rebuilt in 1938 with Walschaert's valve gear and piston valves and with a streamlined front. In 1943−4 it was again rebuilt, as a 4−6−2. (The Science Museum, London)

British Railways Class 5 4−6−0 No 44767 fitted with Stephenson's (Howe's) Link Motion in place of the normal Walschaert's valve gear. Photographed at Bolton on 5 November 1963. (John Marshall)

The only remaining Ramsbottom locomotive, 0–4–0 saddle tank No 1439, built by the London & North Western Railway in 1865, photographed at Highley on the Severn Valley Railway on 9 May 1983. (John Marshall)

Stratford & Moreton Railway wagon and section of track at Stratford on Avon, 5 July 1983. The railway was laid out by John Urpeth Rastrick and opened in 1836. (John Marshall)

**GRAY, John,** 1810–54. First engineer to use the balanced slide valve on locomotives, on the Liverpool & Manchester Railway in 1838. In 1839 he fitted a valve gear to the L & M *Cyclops* designed to utilise the expansion of steam. He was the first engineer to use a long-travel valve motion, about 152 mm (6 in), on the Hull & Selby Railway in 1840. He was among the first to discard the idea of a low centre of gravity as necessary for the safe running of locomotives.

**GREATHEAD, James Henry,** 1844–96. Inventor of the tunnelling shield used in the construction of the London 'tube' railways, first tried in the Tower Subway in 1869–70.

**GREENLY, Henry** 1876–1947. Born at Birkenhead, England. Pioneer of miniature passenger-carrying railways. He engineered the Ravenglass & Eskdale 381 mm (15 in) gauge railway in 1922 and was responsible for the civil engineering and the design of locomotives and rolling stock for the 15 in gauge Romney, Hythe & Dymchurch Railway 1926–30.

**GRESLEY, Sir (Herbert) Nigel,** 1876–1941. Chief mechanical engineer, Great Northern and London & North Eastern Railways. He was trained on the London & North Western Railway at Crewe and the Lancashire & Yorkshire Railway at Horwich. Appointed carriage and wagon superintendent on the GNR at Doncaster in 1905, succeeding H. A. Ivatt (qv) as CME in 1911. After the grouping in 1923 (see p53) he continued as CME of the LNER. He was a progressive locomotive engineer, producing many classes of locomotives which gave long and reliable service. He is most famous for his series of 'Pacifics', culminating in the A4 class of which No 4468 *Mallard* achieved the world's record speed for a steam locomotive of 201.8 km/h (125 mph) in 1938.

**HACKWORTH, Timothy,** 1786–1850. British Steam locomotive pioneer; the first engineer to establish the steam locomotive as a thoroughly reliable machine. He was appointed to take charge of locomotives on the Stockton & Darlington Railway and established a locomotive works at New Shildon on the S & D in 1825. In 1827 he built the first six-coupled locomotive, *Royal George*, the first on which the cylinders drove directly onto the wheels. In 1829 he entered the 0–4–0 *Sans Pareil* for the Rainhill competition on the Liverpool & Manchester Railway but it had to be withdrawn because of a cracked cylinder. It is preserved at the Science Museum, London. He resigned the S & D contract in 1840 and continued in private practice at Shildon. His last locomotive, 2–2–2 *Sans Pareil* (No 2) in 1854, gave good service on the York, Newcastle & Berwick Railway until 1881.

**HAWKSHAW, Sir John,** 1811–91. Civil engineer responsible for many of the most difficult lines of the Lancashire & Yorkshire Railway in the Yorkshire Pennines, 1850–2. From 1865 he was engineer to the East London Railway utilising Marc Brunel's Thames Tunnel of 1842. His greatest work was the completion of the Severn Tunnel, 1879–87, in conjunction with T. A. Walker (qv).

**HEDLEY, William,** 1779–1843. Early British locomotive engineer, one of the first to establish, in 1812, that adequate adhesion could be obtained with smooth wheels on a smooth rail and that the rack used by Blenkinsop (qv) was not necessary. He built his first locomotive at Wylam, Northumberland, in 1813 and a more successful one in 1814. Two of his locomotives, much rebuilt, are preserved: *Wylam Dilly* at

Edinburgh Museum, and *Puffing Billy* at the Science Museum, London. His work undoubtedly influenced George Stephenson who, however, never acknowledged his debt to Hedley.

**HOLDEN, James,** 1837–1925. Locomotive engineer on the Great Eastern Railway, England, 1885–1907. He was responsible for the introduction of 11 classes of sound, simple and economical locomotives, his last the 'Claud Hamilton' class 4–4–0 in 1900. He pioneered the use of oil fuel for locomotives in 1887. In 1902 he produced a large 0–10–0 tank engine, the first British ten-coupled type, to establish the ability of steam locomotives to accelerate as fast as an electric train, thereby defeating a rival railway electrification project.

**HOWE, William,** 1814–79. Designer of the valve gear known as 'Stephenson's Link Motion', first fitted to a 2–4–0 built by Robert Stephenson & Co, Newcastle-upon-Tyne, for the North Midland Railway in 1842.

**HUDSON, George,** 1800–71. Railway promoter and financier of York who guided the progress of the Midland and York & North Midland Railways, amassing a vast fortune in the process. The uncovering of unscrupulous dealings in 1845 led to his downfall.

**IVATT, Henry Alfred,** 1851–1923. Locomotive engineer of the Great Southern & Western Railway, Ireland, from 1886 until 1896 when he became chief mechanical engineer of the Great Northern Railway at Doncaster. In 1898 he introduced Britain's first 4–4–2 or 'Atlantic' type locomotive, No 990 *Henry Oakley* (preserved at the National Railway Museum, York). He retired in 1911, to be succeeded by Gresley (qv).

**JAMES, William,** 1771–1837. Early British railway surveyor and projector. As early as 1803 he surveyed a railway between Liverpool and Manchester. In 1809 he engineered a short plateway between Gloucester and Cheltenham. In 1821 he surveyed the railway from Stratford-on-Avon to Moreton-in-Marsh. This 4 ft-gauge line was built by Rastrick (qv) using wrought-iron rails in chairs and was opened in 1826. He surveyed numerous other railways but was never able to focus his attention on one project sufficiently to see it through to completion. So other engineers received the credit for much of his pioneering work.

**JESSOP, William,** 1745–1814. Builder of canals and early railways and one of the founders of the Butterley Company in Derbyshire (1790). This company later built many iron railway bridges. Most of his railways were built in connection with canals, but in 1801–2 he was chief engineer of the Surrey Iron Railway and, with his son Josias (1781–1826) as assistant, of the Croydon, Merstham & Godstone Railway 1803–5.

**JOY, David,** 1825–1903. Marine and locomotive engineer, trained at

Leeds, England, where, with John Fenton in 1846–7, he designed the famous 'Jenny Lind' type 2–2–2, one of the most successful express passenger engines of the period. He is best remembered as the inventor of the 'Joy' radial valve gear (1879), widely used on the Lancashire & Yorkshire and London & North Western Railways.

**JUDAH, Theodore Dehone,** 1826–63. Driving force and engineer of the Central Pacific Railroad through the Sierra Nevada, California, which made possible the first trans-continental railway route in North America. He died of typhoid contracted while crossing the Isthmus, 6 years before the trans-continental railway was completed.

**KIRTLEY, Matthew,** 1813–73. British locomotive engineer. First Midland Railway locomotive superintendent, from 1844. By the time of his death in office he had increased the locomotive stock from about 100 to 1050. Some of his locomotives, though much rebuilt, lasted into the nationalised British Railways era and one, 2–4–0 No 158A, is preserved at the Midland Railway Centre at Butterley, Derbyshire. Kirtley was the first locomotive engineer to combine the firebox brick arch and the firehole deflector plate, for burning coal instead of coke. He was one of the founder members of the Institution of Mechanical Engineers in 1847.

**LENTZ, Dr Hugo,** 1859–1944. Inventor of the poppet valve gear which he first applied in 1900 to a stationary steam engine built at his works at Brno, Czechoslovakia. Its first use on a locomotive was on one built by Hanomag, Hannover, in 1902, using vertical valves. In 1907 he brought out his gear with horizontal valves operated by oscillating cams. Both these worked from normal valve gear. His third design, 1921, used rotary cams. This gear was used in Britain by Gresley. Two more designs followed and by the time of his death about 2000 locomotives had been fitted with Lentz poppet valve gear.

**LOCKE, Joseph,** 1805–60. One of the leading British railway civil engineers of his time, responsible for building the Grand Junction Railway (Warrington–Birmingham), and railways in France and Spain. In 1840 he took J. E. Errington into partnership and together they built the West Coast main line from Preston to Glasgow and Edinburgh, completed 1848. Locke was noted for economy of railway construction and avoidance of tunnels.

**MACKENZIE, William,** 1794–1851. Important British railway contractor, beginning with Lime Street tunnel at Liverpool (1836) and the Grand Junction Railway (1837). With Brassey (qv) he carried out much railway construction in France and with John Stephenson he built the line from Preston to Glasgow and Edinburgh, and other lines, for Locke and Errington (qqv).

**McNEILL, William Gibbs, 1801–53.** Pioneer civil engineer of railroads in the USA. Worked in close association with G. W. Whistler (qv) who later married his sister. Alone or with Whistler he was engaged on many early railroads in the Eastern States of USA, including the Baltimore & Ohio.

**MALLET, Anatole, 1837–1919.** French locomotive engineer. Inventor of the Mallet articulated compound steam locomotive, patented in 1884, consisting of a fixed rear engine unit carrying the high-pressure cylinders and a swivelling front engine unit carrying the low-pressure cylinders. In its simple-expansion form the Mallet developed into the world's largest steam locomotives, the Union Pacific 4–8–8–4 'Big Boys'.

**MANSON, James, 1845–1935.** Locomotive superintendent of the Great North of Scotland Railway (1883–90) and the Glasgow & South Western Railway (1890–1911). He is best remembered as inventor of the automatic tablet exchanger for single-line working (1886).

**MURRAY, Matthew, 1765–1826.** Mechanical engineer of Leeds, England; builder of the first commercially successful steam locomotives in 1811–13 using Blenkinsop's (qv) rack system for the Middleton Colliery Railway. He is credited with invention of the short 'D' slide valve which he patented in 1802.

**PEACOCK, Richard, 1820–89.** At the age of only 18 he was appointed locomotive superintendent on the Leeds & Selby Railway, England. From 1841 he held the same office on the nearly completed Sheffield, Ashton & Manchester Railway and was responsible for establishing the locomotive works at Gorton, Manchester. In 1854 he went into partnership with Charles Beyer (qv) and together they founded the famous locomotive building firm of Beyer Peacock & Co at Gorton, builders of steam locomotives for railways throughout the world.

**PEASE, Edward, 1767–1858.** Promoter of the Stockton & Darlington Railway and supporter of George Stephenson in his early years as a railway engineer. One of the founders of Robert Stephenson & Co, locomotive manufacturers of Newcastle-upon-Tyne, in 1823.

**PETO, Sir Samuel Morton, 1809–89.** Important British railway contractor and civil engineer. With Thomas Grissell (1801–74) he built part of the Great Western Railway as well as the new Houses of Parliament; with E. L. Betts (qv) the Great Northern 'Loop Line' through Boston (1847–8), the Oxford, Worcester & Wolverhampton Railway (1850–4), and the GWR Oxford–Birmingham (1850–2); and with Brassey (qv) many railways abroad. He was chairman of the Chester & Holyhead Railway 1851–9. In 1854 he was awarded a baronetcy for his work on the railway in the Crimea which he carried out without profit to himself.

**PULLMAN, George Mortimer, 1831–97.** Founder of the Pullman Car

Company in the USA. He built his first car in 1865. The Pullman Car was introduced to Britain by the Midland Railway in 1874.

**RAMSBOTTOM, John,** 1814–97. Locomotive superintendent in England, first on the Manchester & Birmingham Railway, 1842–57, then on the LNWR at Crewe, 1857–71. His numerous inventions included the Ramsbottom safety valve, and the water trough and pick-up apparatus.

**RASTRICK, John Urpeth,** 1780–1856. British civil and mechanical engineer. In association with Hazeldine of Bridgnorth, Shropshire, he was involved in the Construction of the world's first steam locomotive (see Trevithick). His first railway work was as engineer on the Stratford & Moreton Railway, 1822–6 (see James). His greatest work was the London–Brighton Railway, opened 1841.

**RIDDLES, Robert Arthur,** 1892–1983. British locomotive engineer, trained at Crewe, LNWR, from 1909. He rose to importance as a locomotive engineer on the London, Midland & Scottish Railway. During World War II, while in charge of the Directorate of Transport at the Ministry of Supply, he was responsible for the design and construction of the 935 2–8–0s and 150 2–10–0s for the War Department. On the formation of British Railways on 1 January 1948 he was placed in charge of mechanical and electrical engineering and he supervised the design of the entire range of BR standard steam locomotives. He retired from BR in 1953, having unsuccessfully recommended full-scale electrification, instead of replacement of steam by diesel traction. Shortly afterwards he became chairman of Stothert & Pitt, crane makers at Bath. He finally retired in 1967.

**SAXBY, John,** 1821–1913. Inventor of the interlocking mechanism between points and signals which he patented in 1856 and first applied on the London, Brighton & South Coast Railway. In 1862, in partnership with J. S. Farmer (1827–92) he formed the firm of Saxby & Farmer for the manufacture of signalling apparatus.

**SCHMIDT, Wilhelm,** 1858–1924. German engineer. Designer and promoter of the high-degree fire-tube superheater which greatly improved the efficiency of steam locomotives. His first superheater was used in 1898; the fire-tube type was first used in Belgium in 1901. Within ten years it was fitted to most large locomotives throughout the world.

**SEGUIN, Marc,** 1786–1875. French pioneer of the multi-tubular boiler which he patented in 1827 and which he used, with a forced draught, on a locomotive in 1828. This was the first locomotive to run on the railway he engineered between Lyons and St Etienne, opened in 1829.

**SIEMENS, Dr Ernst Werner von,** 1816–92. Builder of the world's first practical electric railway, at Berlin in 1879. His brother William

37

(1823—83) built the Giant's Causeway Tramway in Ireland (1883), one of the earliest electric railways in the British Isles.

**SPOONER, Charles Easton,** 1818—89. Engineer of the Festiniog Railway in Wales and pioneer of narrow-gauge steam locomotives. From the age of 14 he assisted his father, James Spooner (1789—1856), in the construction of the railway and from 1856 became manager and engineer. He introduced steam locomotives in 1863.

**SPRAGUE, Frank Julian,** 1857—1934. Pioneer of electric traction in the USA, beginning with street cars in 1887. In 1895 he perfected his system of multiple-unit control for electric trains without locomotives.

**STANIER, Sir William Arthur, FRS,** 1876—1965. Locomotive engineer. Trained at Swindon, GWR, remaining with that railway until 1932 when he was appointed chief mechanical engineer of the London Midland & Scottish Railway. Here he revolutionised the locomotive department with a few standard types in large classes. His 'Class 5' 4—6—0 (1934) and '8F' 2—8—0 (1935) were among the last steam locomotive types on British Railways.

**STEPHENSON, George,** 1781—1848. As a boy, with almost no education, he worked on colliery engines at Wylam, Northumberland, at the same time learning to read and write. He took a close interest in the locomotives working on the Wylam wagonway and in 1814 he built his first locomotive. In 1815, besides inventing a miner's safety lamp, he patented a locomotive in which the exhaust steam was used to draw the fire. He supervised construction and equipping of the Hetton Colliery Railway, 1819—22, and was then appointed engineer to the Stockton & Darlington Railway, opened 1925. This established his reputation and led to his appointment as engineer to the Liverpool & Manchester Railway, opened in 1830, followed by the Leicester & Swannington (1832), Birmingham & Derby (1839), North Midland and York & North Midland (1840), Manchester & Leeds (1841) and other railways. In 1823, with Edward Pease (qv) and others, he established a locomotive works in Newcastle under the name of his son, Robert Stephenson & Co.

**STEPHENSON, Robert,** 1803—59. Son of George, who made certain that Robert had as good an education as possible. In 1823 he took up management of the locomotive works of Robert Stephenson & Co but had to leave England to recover his health, which was never completely sound. He spent some time in Colombia, South America; returned 1827 and became involved in the dispute over motive power for the Liverpool & Manchester Railway of which his father was engineer. Robert was largely responsible for the design of *Rocket* which won the Rainhill prize in 1829. He was engineer of the London & Birmingham Railway 1833—8.

He is best remembered for his great bridges, particularly the High Level Bridge at Newcastle-upon-Tyne, 1846–9. With William Fairbairn (qv) he evolved the form of wrought-iron tubular girder used at Conway (1847–9), Menai Strait (1847–50), and near Montreal (1854–9).

STEVENS, John, 1749–1838. Pioneer of mechanical transport in the USA, and builder of the first American steam locomotive (1825) which ran on a track on his private estate at Hoboken, NJ. His earlier career was concerned with steamships.

SYKES, William Robert, 1840–1917. Inventor of the 'lock and block' signalling system. He began his railway career with the London, Brighton & South Coast Railway in 1863. He introduced track circuiting in 1864. His lock and block system was patented in 1875, and was introduced in the USA in 1882. In 1899 he left railway service and formed the W. R. Sykes Interlocking Signal Company.

TREVITHICK, Richard, 1771–1833. Pioneer in the use of high-pressure steam and builder of the first steam railway locomotives. In 1800–1 he built a steam carriage. His first railway locomotive was built at Coalbrookdale, Shropshire, in 1803 for the 914 mm (3 ft) gauge plateway, but there is no proof that it ever ran. In 1804 he built a locomotive for the Penydarren Ironworks near Merthyr Tydfil in South Wales which pulled a load of 10 tons of iron and 70 men. A third, built at Gateshead near Newcastle in 1805, was the first to have flanged wheels. After demonstrating another on a circular track in London his failure to interest anyone in steam locomotives caused him to turn his attention to the development of stationary engines.

TYER, Edward, 1830–1912. British signalling engineer. Responsible for numerous inventions in the development of block signalling and the tablet system (1878) for single-line operation.

VAN HORNE, Sir William Cornelius, 1843–1915. Railway executive, born in the USA, and the driving force behind the construction of the Canadian Pacific Railway, 1881–6. He was president of the CPR 1888–99.

VAUCLAIN, Samuel Matthews, 1856–1940. Chairman of Baldwin Locomotive Works, USA, and inventor of the system of locomotive compounding named after him in which the high and low pressure piston rods on both sides of the engine were connected to common crossheads. From 1891 to 1905 about 2000 were built.

VIGNOLES, Charles Blacker, 1793–1875. British civil engineer. Chief engineer of the Sheffield–Manchester Railway including the first Wood-head tunnel, 1835–8. In 1837 he introduced the flat-bottomed rail named after him, similar in section to that invented by R. L. Stevens (1787–1856) in the USA.

**VOLK, Magnus,** 1851–1937. Engineer of the Volk's Electric Railway in Brighton (1883), the first electric railway in Britain; and also of the extraordinary Brighton & Rottingdean Seashore Electric Tramway (1896–1901).

**WALKER, Thomas Andrew,** 1828–89. Civil engineer and contractor who worked on some of the most difficult railway engineering projects in Britain, including the East London through Marc Brunel's Thames Tunnel (1876) and the completion of the Severn Tunnel (1879–87), and also docks and the Manchester Ship Canal.

**WALSCHAERT, Egide,** 1820–1901. Belgian locomotive engineer, famous for the design (1844) of his valve gear, first applied to a locomotive in Belgium, in 1848. It was first used in Britain on a Fairlie 0–6–6–0 on the East & West Junction Railway in 1876.

**WESTINGHOUSE, George,** 1846–1914. American Inventor, designer of the Westinghouse air brake, and manufacturer. The non-automatic 'straight air' brake was patented in 1868. The automatic brake was developed in 1872–3.

**WHISTLER, George Washington,** 1800–49. Pioneer railway engineer in the USA. With W. G. McNeill (qv) he laid out the Baltimore & Ohio Railroad and other early railways in the USA. In 1842 he laid out the railway from Moscow to St Petersburg (now Leningrad), adopting the 5 ft gauge then standard in his native Southern States and which thus became the standard gauge in Russia. While engaged in its construction he contracted cholera and died a year before the railway was completed.

**WORSDELL, Nathaniel,** 1809–76. Inventor and carriage builder, responsible for building the first carriages for the Liverpool & Manchester Railway in 1830. He established the form of the compartment coach by fitting three horse carriage bodies on a railway truck (1838). In 1837 he invented an apparatus for picking up and depositing mail bags. He also designed a screw coupling, but with a single right-hand thread only.

**WORSDELL, Thomas William,** 1838–1916. Locomotive engineer, Great Eastern and North Eastern Railways, England. Son of Nathaniel. While on the NER he developed his two-cylinder compound principle, an example of which can be seen on the 2–2–4 tank *Aerolite* at the National Railway Museum, York.

# 3 Principal Railway Systems of the World

| System | Date of first line | Gauge mm | ft | in | Route length km | miles |
|--------|------|------|------|------|------|------|
| **ARGENTINA** | | | | | | |
| Argentine Railways (Ferrocarriles Argentinos) | 1857 | | | | | |
| *Divisions:* | | | | | | |
| Roca | | 1 676 | 5 | 6 | 7 977 | 4 957 |
| | | 750 | 2 | 5½ | 285 | 177 |
| Mitre | | 1 676 | 5 | 6 | 5 942 | 3 692 |
| San Martin | | 1 676 | 5 | 6 | 4 625 | 2 874 |
| Sarmiento | | 1 676 | 5 | 6 | 3 557 | 2 210 |
| Urquiza | | 1 435 | 4 | 8½ | 3 088 | 1 919 |
| Belgrano | | 1 000 | 3 | 3⅜ | 11 844 | 7 359 |
| TOTAL, all gauges | | | | | 37 318 | 23 188 |
| **AUSTRALIA** | | | | | | |
| New South Wales | 1855 | | | | 10 148 | 6 306[1] |
| Victoria | 1854 | | | | 5 856 | 3 638 |
| Queensland | 1865 | | | | 9 789 | 6 082 |
| South Australia | 1856 | | | | 5 944 | 3 693 |
| Western Australia | 1879 | | | | 6 501 | 4 040 |
| Tasmania | 1871 | | | | 864 | 537 |
| Northern Territory | 1889 | | | | 278 | 173 |
| Australian Capital Territory | | | | | 8 | 5 |
| TOTAL AUSTRALIA (30 June 1979) | | | | | 39 388 | 24 475 |

[1] The Australian route lengths include lines of 1600 mm, 1435 mm and 1067 mm gauges, and Australian national Railways lines in each state. (For more detail see pp 113–134.)

| System | Date of first line | Gauge mm | ft | in | Route length km | miles |
|---|---|---|---|---|---|---|
| **BRAZIL** | 1854 | | | | | |
| Brazilian Federal | | | | | | |
| Railways | | 1 600 | 5 | 3 | 1 736 | 1 079 |
| (Rêde Ferroviaria | | 1 000 | 3 | $3\frac{3}{8}$ | 21 711 | 13 490 |
| Federal SA) | | 762 | 2 | 6 | 202 | 126 |
| TOTAL, all gauges | | | | | 23 649 | 14 695 |
| São Paulo Railway | | 1 000 | 3 | $3\frac{3}{8}$ | 3 619 | 2 249 |
| | | 1 600 | 5 | 3 | 1 650 | 1 025 |
| TOTAL | | | | | 5 269 | 3 274 |
| | | | | | | |
| **CANADA** | 1836 | | | | | |
| Algoma Central Railway | | 1 435 | 4 | $8\frac{1}{2}$ | 516 | 321 |
| British Columbia | | | | | | |
| Railway | | 1 435 | 4 | $8\frac{1}{2}$ | 2 017 | 1 253 |
| Canadian National | | 1 435 | 4 | $8\frac{1}{2}$ | 38 454 | 23 894 |
| Railways | | 1 067 | 3 | 6 | 1 146 | 712 |
| Canadian Pacific | | | | | | |
| Railway | | 1 435 | 4 | $8\frac{1}{2}$ | 26 397 | 16 402 |
| Quebec, North Shore | | | | | | |
| & Labrador Railway | | 1 435 | 4 | $8\frac{1}{2}$ | 639 | 397 |
| White Pass & Yukon | | 915 | 3 | 0 | 178 | 111 |
| TOTAL, all gauges | | | | | 69 340 | 43 086 |
| | | | | | | |
| **CHILE** | 1851 | 1 676 | 5 | 6 | 4 274 | 2 655 |
| | | 1 435 | 4 | $8\frac{1}{2}$ | 235 | 146 |
| | | 1 000 | 3 | $3\frac{3}{8}$ | 3 300 | 2 050 |
| | | 1 676 | 5 | 6 | 8 | 5 |
| | | 1 000[1] | 3 | $3\frac{3}{8}$ | | |
| | | 1 435 | 4 | $8\frac{1}{2}$ | 135 | 84 |
| | | 1 000[1] | 3 | $3\frac{3}{8}$ | | |
| TOTAL, all gauges | | | | | 7 952 | 4 941 |

[1] Dual gauge.

| System | Date of first line | Gauge | | | Route length | |
|---|---|---|---|---|---|---|
| | | mm | ft | in | km | miles |
| **CHINA** | 1880 | | | | | |
| Chinese Peoples' Republic Railways (Building about 1000 km a year of new route. Aims to achieve 80 000 km by 2000.) | | 1 435 | 4 | $8\frac{1}{2}$ | c 50 000 | c 31 000 |
| **CZECHOSLOVAKIA** | 1839 | 1 435 | 4 | $8\frac{1}{2}$ | 13 029 | 8 095 |
| | | 1 524 | 5 | 0 | 102 | 63 |
| **FRANCE** | 1832 | 1 435 | 4 | $8\frac{1}{2}$ | 34 362 | 21 351 |
| **GERMANY** | 1835 | | | | | |
| German Federal Railways (DB) | | 1 435 | 4 | $8\frac{1}{2}$ | 28 450 | 17 678 |
| German State Railways (DR) | | 1 435 | 4 | $8\frac{1}{2}$ | 14 215 | 8 833 |
| TOTAL | | | | | 42 665 | 26 511 |
| **GREAT BRITAIN** | 1830[2] | 1 435 | 4 | $8\frac{1}{2}$ | 17 229 | 10 706 |
| | | 600 | 1 | $11\frac{5}{8}$ | 19 | 12 |

[2] 1830 was the year of opening of the Liverpool & Manchester Railway, the first 'modern' railway. There were already many miles of railway in operation in Great Britain before this.

| | | | | | | |
|---|---|---|---|---|---|---|
| **INDIA** | 1853 | | | | | |
| *Zonal Administrative Units:* | | | | | | |
| Central Railway (Bombay) | | 1 676 | 5 | 6 | 4 840 | 3 007 |
| | | 1 000 | 3 | $3\frac{3}{8}$ | 382 | 237 |
| | | 762 | 2 | 6 | 367 | 228 |
| | | 610 | 2 | 0 | 303 | 188 |
| TOTAL | | | | | 5 892 | 3 660 |

| System | Date of first line | Gauge | | | Route length km | miles |
|--------|------|-----|-----|-----|-----|-----|
| | | mm | ft | in | | |

**India** (cont.)

| | | | | | | |
|--------|------|-----|-----|-----|-----|-----|
| Eastern Railway | | 1 676 | 5 | 6 | 4 070 | 2 529 |
| (Calcutta) | | 762 | 2 | 6 | 132 | 82 |
| TOTAL | | | | | 4 202 | 6 261 |
| | | | | | | |
| Northern Railway | | 1 676 | 5 | 6 | 6 998 | 4 348 |
| (Delhi) | | 1 000 | 3 | $3\frac{3}{8}$ | 3 430 | 2 131 |
| | | 762 | 2 | 6 | 260 | 161 |
| TOTAL | | | | | 10 688 | 6 640 |
| | | | | | | |
| North Eastern Railway | | 1 676 | 5 | 6 | 755 | 469 |
| (Gorakhpur, UP) | | 1 000 | 3 | $3\frac{3}{8}$ | 4 358 | 2 708 |
| TOTAL | | | | | 5 113 | 3 177 |
| | | | | | | |
| North East Frontier | | 1 676 | 5 | 6 | 803 | 499 |
| Railway (Assam) | | 1 000 | 3 | $3\frac{3}{8}$ | 2 737 | 1 700 |
| | | 610 | 2 | 0 | 87 | 54 |
| TOTAL | | | | | 3 627 | 2 253 |
| | | | | | | |
| Southern (Madras) | | 1 676 | 5 | 6 | 2 562 | 1 592 |
| | | 1 000 | 3 | $3\frac{3}{8}$ | 4 871 | 3 027 |
| | | 762 | 2 | 6 | 148 | 92 |
| TOTAL | | | | | 7 581 | 4 711 |
| | | | | | | |
| South Central Railway | | 1 676 | 5 | 6 | 3 165 | 1 967 |
| (Secunderabad) | | 1 000 | 3 | $3\frac{3}{8}$ | 3 313 | 2 058 |
| TOTAL | | | | | 6 478 | 4 025 |
| | | | | | | |
| South Eastern Railway | | 1 676 | 5 | 6 | 5 511 | 3 424 |
| (Calcutta) | | 762 | 2 | 6 | 1 479 | 919 |
| TOTAL | | | | | 6 990 | 4 343 |

| System | Date of first line | Gauge | | | Route length | |
|---|---|---|---|---|---|---|
| | | mm | ft | in | km | miles |
| Western Railway (Bombay) | | 1 676 | 5 | 6 | 3 085 | 1 917 |
| | | 1 000 | 3 | 3⅜ | 6 118 | 3 802 |
| | | 762 | 2 | 6 | 1 135 | 705 |
| TOTAL | | | | | 10 338 | 6 424 |
| TOTALS | | 1 676 | 5 | 6 | 31 789 | 19 753 |
| | | 1 000 | 3 | 3⅜ | 25 209 | 15 664 |
| | | 762 | 2 | 6 | 3 521 | 2 188 |
| | | 610 | 2 | 0 | 390 | 242 |
| TOTAL, all gauges | | | | | 60 909 | 37 847 |
| **ITALY** | 1839 | 1 435 | 4 | 8½ | 16 133 | 10 024 |
| **JAPAN** | 1872 | 1 435 | 4 | 8½ | 1177 | 731 |
| | | 1 067 | 3 | 6 | 20 145 | 12 517 |
| TOTAL, both gauges | | | | | 21 322 | 13 248 |
| **MEXICO** | 1850 | 914 | 3 | 0 | 451 | 280 |
| | | 1 435 | 4 | 8½ | 14 151 | 8 793 |
| | | Mixed gauge | | | 72 | 45 |
| TOTAL | | | | | 14 674 | 9 118 |
| **PAKISTAN** | 1861 | 1 675 | 5 | 6 | 7 754 | 4 818 |
| | | 1 000 | 3 | 3⅜ | 444 | 276 |
| | | 762 | 2 | 6 | 610 | 379 |
| TOTAL | | | | | 8 808 | 5 473 |
| **POLAND** | 1842 | 1 435 | 4 | 8½ | 23 855 | 14 822 |
| **ROUMANIA** | 1869 | 1 435 | 4 | 8½ | 10 515 | 6 534 |
| | | 610 | 2 | 0 | 568 | 353 |
| | | 762 | 2 | 6 | | |
| TOTAL | | | | | 11 083 | 6 887 |

| System | Date of first line | Gauge | | | Route length | |
|---|---|---|---|---|---|---|
| | | mm | ft | in | km | miles |
| **SOUTH AFRICA** | 1860 | 1 065 | 3 | 6 | 22 891 | 14 223 |
| | | 610 | 2 | 0 | 705 | 438 |
| TOTAL | | | | | 23 596 | 14 661 |
| **SPAIN** | 1848 | 1 668 | 5 | 6 | 13 531 | 8 407 |
| **SWEDEN** | 1856 | 1 435 | 4 | 8½ | 11 158 | 6 933 |
| | | 891 | 2 | 11 | 182 | 113 |
| TOTAL | | | | | 11 340 | 7 046 |

The Norwegian iron-ore terminal at Narvik, north of the Arctic Circle, 1 May 1979 (John Marshall)

| System | Date of first line | Gauge | | | Route length km | miles |
|--------|--------------------|-------|---|-----|------------------|-------|
| | | mm | ft | in | | |
| **TURKEY** | 1896 | 1 435 | 4 | 8½ | 8 140 | 5 857 |
| **USA** (for details see p 89) | 1830 | 1 435 | 4 | 8½ | 294 625 | 183 077 |
| **USSR** | 1837 | 1 520 | 4 | 11 | c 140 000 | c 87 100 |
| | | 600 } | 2 | 11⅝ } | 2 718 | 1 689 |
| | | 1 000 } | 3 | 3⅜ } | | |
| | | 1 435 | 4 | 8½ | 75 | 47 |
| TOTAL, all gauges | | | | | c 142 993 | c 88 836 |
| **YUGOSLAVIA** | 1846 | 1 435 | 4 | 8½ | 9 762 | 6 066 |

One of the oldest engines on the Turkish State Railways, 0–6–0 No 33 508, built by Hanomag of Hannover in 1872. It is scheduled for preservation. (John Marshall)

The countries with the largest railway systems are USA, USSR, Canada, India/Pakistan/Bangladesh,[1] and China. Their developments were as follows:

| | 1840 km miles | 1860 km miles | 1880 km miles | 1900 km miles | 1920 km miles | 1940 km miles | 1960 km miles | 1980 km miles |
|---|---|---|---|---|---|---|---|---|
| USA | 4 535 2 818 | 49 288 30 626 | 150 100 93 267 | 311 187 193 366 | 406 941 252 865 | 376 880 234 182 | 350 114 217 552 | 294 626 183 077 |
| USSR | 27 17 | 1 077 669 | 17 708 11 003 | 44 492 27 646 | 71 597 44 488 | 106 105 65 930 | 125 789 78 164 | 141 800 88 110 |
| CANADA | 26 16 | 3 324 2 065 | 11 577 7 194 | 28 415 17 657 | 63 382 39 384 | 68 502 42 565 | 70 858 44 029 | 69 340 43 086 |
| INDIA/ PAKISTAN/ BANGLADESH[1] | | 1 349 838 | 14 744 9 162 | 39 835 24 752 | 59 119 36 734 | 66 234 41 156 | 68 002 42 254 | 72 591 45 106 |
| CHINA | | | | 2 346 1 458 | 11 189 6 952 | 31 382 19 500 | c 50 000 c 31 000 | |

[1] India, Pakistan and Bangladesh are taken for this purpose as one geographical unit for which the railways were laid out before partition.

48

Turkish State Railways heavy freight train from Erzincan to Erzurum at Altunkent on 17 April 1983, headed by 2–10–0s Nos 56 546 and 56 121. (John Marshall)

The Viso zigzag at 112 km on the Peru Central Railway. The upper level can be seen in the centre of the photograph. (John Marshall)

An example of engineering on the Peru Central Railway. Infiernillo Bridge, 5 October 1974. (John Marshall)

The oldest engine in Argentina, at Monte Caseros on 22 October 1974, was 0–6–0 No 20 on the standard-gauge Urquiza system. It was built by Neilson Reid at Glasgow in 1888. (John Marshall)

Japanese 1676 mm (5 ft 6 in) gauge 4–8–2 No 859 at Temuco, Chile, on 17 October 1974. Built by Mitsubishi in 1952. (John Marshall)

Metre-gauge 4–8–2 No 814, built by Vulcan Foundry, Lancashire, in 1954, at Oruro, Bolivia, on 11 October 1974. (John Marshall)

Metre-gauge 2–8–2 No 662, built by Hitachi, Japan, in 1958, at Condor, Bolivia, on 8 October 1974. This is the world's highest railway station, 4787 m (15 705 ft). (John Marshall)

The Chile end of the summit tunnel at La Cumbre on the metre-gauge Transandine Railway, photographed on 19 October 1974. Passenger services were withdrawn in 1979. (John Marshall)

# 4 British Railways

From 1801 to 1914 a total of 1279 separate British companies were incorporated, or existing companies were authorised, by Acts of Parliament to build railways in mainland Britain. Many of these, because of failure to raise sufficient capital, or for other reasons, never built the railways that were authorised. From 1834 when the North Union Railway was formed by the amalgamation of the Wigan Branch and Wigan & Preston Railways by the first Railway Amalgamation Act, a steady process of amalgamations kept the number of separate companies down. In 1851 there were 147 and at the end of 1922 there were 168. Many of these were leased or worked by larger companies.

After World War I the British government, which earlier had ruled out a

Length of Liverpool & Manchester Railway wrought-iron rail and stone sleepers, probably dating from 1830, at Edge Hill Station Museum, Liverpool, 25 May 1980. (John Marshall)

number of major amalgamation schemes because of a fear of monopolies, and which had taken over the railways during the war, now decided that they could be operated more efficiently and economically if they were further amalgamated. Under the Railways Act, 19 August 1921 (Ch 55), 123 separate companies were amalgamated into four groups. The remaining 45 companies, mostly minor concerns, carried on under their old names. The four groups were described in the Act as: 1 The Southern Group; 2 The Western Group; 3 The North Western, Midland and West Scottish Group; 4 the North Eastern and East Scottish Group.

The 'grouping' came into force on 1 January 1923. The four railway companies became known as:

1 The Great Western Railway; 2 The London, Midland & Scottish Railway; 3 The London & North Eastern Railway; 4 The Southern Railway. They were made up as follows:

## GREAT WESTERN RAILWAY

| Company | Owned | Share of joint lines | Lines leased or worked | Share of lines leased or worked jointly | Total route |
|---|---|---|---|---|---|
| | km miles | km miles | km miles | km miles | km miles |
| Old GWR | 4 278 | 203.7 | 312.5 | 42.2 | 4 836.4 |
| | 2 658 | 126.6 | 194.2 | 26.2 | 3 005 |
| Barry Railway | 76 | | 33.3 | | 109.3 |
| | 47.2 | | 20.7 | | 67.9 |
| Cambrian Railways | 388.3 | | 62.8 | | 475.2 |
| | 241.3 | | 39 | | 295.3 |
| Cardiff Railway | 18.5 | 0.4 | | | 18.9 |
| | 11.5 | 0.25 | | | 11.75 |
| Midland & South | 97.7 | | 3.85 | | 101.5 |
| Western Junction R | 60.7 | | 2.4 | | 63.1 |
| Rhymney Railway | 62 | 16.3 | 2.4 | 1.4 | 82 |
| | 38.5 | 10.15 | 1.5 | 0.9 | 51 |
| Taff Vale Railway | 180.2 | 0.4 | 19.7 | | 200.35 |
| | 112 | 0.25 | 12.25 | | 124.5 |

## Subsidiary Companies

| Company | Worked by | km | miles |
|---|---|---|---|
| Brecon & Merthyr Tydfil Junction | | 96.2 | 59.8 |
| Bury Port & Gwendreath Valley | | 33.8 | 21 |
| Cleobury Mortimer & Ditton Priors Light Railway | | 19.3 | 12 |
| Didcot, Newbury & Southampton R (Newbury and Winchester sections) | GWR | 67.5 | 42 |
| Exeter Railway | GWR | 14 | 8.75 |
| Forest of Dean Central Railway | GWR | 8 | 5 |
| Gwendreath Valleys Railway | | 4.8 | 3 |
| Lampeter, Aberayon & New Quay Light Railway | GWR | 19.3 | 12 |
| Liskeard & Looe Railway | GWR | 14.5 | 9 |
| Llanelly & Mynydd Mawr Railway | | 20.9 | 13 |
| Mawddy Railway | Cambrian | 10.9 | 6.75 |
| Neath & Brecon Railway | | 64.4 | 40 |
| Penarth Extension | Taff Vale | 2 | 1.25 |
| Penarth Harbour, Docks & Railway | Taff Vale | 14.9 | 9.25 |
| Port Talbot Railway & Docks | | 56.3 | 35 |
| Princetown Railway | GWR | 16.9 | 10.5 |
| Rhondda & Swansea Bay | | 46.3 | 28.8 |
| Ross & Monmouth Railway | GWR | 20.1 | 12.5 |
| South Wales Mineral Railway | Port Talbot R | 20.9 | 13 |
| Teign Valley Railway | GWR | 12.5 | 7.75 |
| Vale of Glamorgan Railway | Barry R | 33.3 | 20.7 |
| Van Railway | Cambrian Rs | 10.9 | 6.75 |
| Welshpool & Llanfair Light Railway (762 mm (2 ft 6 in) gauge) | Cambrian Rs | 14.5 | 9 |
| West Somerset Railway | GWR | 23.3 | 14.5 |
| Wrexham & Ellesmere Railway | Cambrian Rs | 20.5 | 12.75 |

Mixed-gauge GWR trackwork being assembled at Didcot, Oxfordshire, 27 May ▶ 1983. (John Marshall)

## Companies Jointly Owned with the GWR

| Company | km | miles |
| --- | --- | --- |
| Quakers Yard & Merthyr (GW & Rhymney) | 9.6 | 6 |
| Taff Bargoed (GW & Rhymney) | 17.7 | 11 |

## Joint with other Grouped Companies

| Company | Joint with | km | miles |
| --- | --- | --- | --- |
| Birkenhead | LMS | 90.9 | 56.5 |
| Brecon & Merthyr & LNW Joint | LMS | 9.6 | 6 |
| Brynmawr & Western Valleys | LMS | 1.8 | 1.1 |
| Clee Hill | LMS | 9.6 | 6 |
| Clifton Extension | LMS | 14.5 | 9 |
| Easton & Church Hope | SR | 5.6 | 3.5 |
| Fishguard & Rosslare Railways & Harbours | GS & W | 169 | 105 |
| GWR & GCR Joint | LNER | 66 | 41 |
| Halesowen | LMS | 9.6 | 6 |
| Hammersmith & City | Met | 4.8 | 3 |
| Nantybwch & Rhymney | LMS | 4.8 | 3 |
| Severn & Wye Joint | LMS | 62.8 | 39 |
| Shrewsbury & Hereford | LMS | 133.2 | 82.75 |
| Tenbury | LMS | 8 | 5 |
| Vale of Towy | LMS | 17.7 | 11 |

| Company | Joint with | km | miles |
|---|---|---|---|
| Victoria Station & Pimlico | To SR | | |
| West London | LMS | 4 | 2.5 |
| West London Extension | SR | 8.2 | 5.1 |
| Weymouth & Portland | SR | 8.8 | 5.5 |
| Wrexham & Minera | LMS | 4.8 | 3 |

## GWR totals at 1 January 1923

| | km | miles |
|---|---|---|
| Owned | 5 869 | 3 647 |
| Share of joint lines | 195.5 | 121.5 |
| Lines leased or worked | 3.86 | 2.4 |
| Share of lines leased or worked jointly | 41.2 | 25.6 |
| TOTAL route | 6 108.1 | 3 795.5 |

| *Rolling stock:* | |
|---|---|
| Tender locomotives | 1 502 |
| Tank locomotives | 2 442 |
| TOTAL locomotives | 3 944 |
| TOTAL carriage stock | 10 139 |
| TOTAL wagons | 86 249 |
| Service vehicles | 9 619 |

Pandrol rail clips on paved concrete track (PACT). (John Marshall)

## LONDON MIDLAND & SCOTTISH RAILWAY

| Company | Owned | Share of joint lines | Lines leased or worked | Share of lines leased or worked jointly | Total route |
|---|---|---|---|---|---|
| | km miles | km miles | km miles | km miles | km miles |
| London & North Western Railway[1] | 3 947.9 2 453.2 | 322.75 200.55 | 76.3 47.4 | 10.8 6.7 | 4 357.8 2 707.9 |
| [1]LNWR included Lancashire & Yorkshire R amalg. 1.1.1922. | 857.8 533 | 109.9 68.3 | | | 967.7 601.3 |
| Midland Railway | 2 460.2 1 528.75 (Britain) 426.9 265.3 (NCC Ireland) | 374.65 232.8 (Britain) 73 45.4 (Co Donegal) | 11.2 7 (Britain) 15.4 9.6 (Co Donegal) | 129.2 80.3 | 3 491 2 169.25 |
| North Staffordshire Railway | 332 206.3 | 9.65 6 | 13.3 8.25 | | 354.3 220.6 |
| Furness Railway | 185 115 | 38.3 23.8 | 31.3 19.45 | | 254.7 158.25 |
| Caledonian Railway | 1 442.7 896.5 | 98.2 61 | 246 152.9 | 6.8 4.25 | 1 793.7 1 114.6 |
| Glasgow & South Western Railway | 722 448.7 | 71.5 44.45 | | 0.5 0.3 | 794.1 493.45 |
| Highland Railway | 780.2 484.8 | | 34.1 21.2 | | 814.3 506 |

## Subsidiary Companies

| Company | Worked by | km | miles |
| --- | --- | --- | --- |
| Arbroath & Forfar | CR | 23.75 | 14.75 |
| Brechin & Edzell District | CR | 10 | 6.25 |
| Callander & Oban | CR | 105.9 | 72 |
| Callander & Ballachulish | CR | 44.7 | 27.75 |
| Cathcart District | | 13.6 | 5.25 |
| Charnwood Forest | LNWR | 16.9 | 10.5 |
| Cleator & Workington Junction | | 49 | 30.5 |
| Cockermouth, Keswick & Penrith | LNWR | 49.6 | 30.8 |
| Dearne Valley | LYR | 33.8 | 21 |
| Dornoch Light | HR | 12.5 | 7.75 |
| Dundee & Newtyle | CR | 23.3 | 14.5 |
| Harborne | LNWR | 4 | 2.5 |
| Killin | CR | 13.6 | 5.25 |
| Knott End | | 18.5 | 11.5 |
| Lanarkshire & Ayrshire | CR | 34.2 | 21.25 |
| Lanarkshire & Ayrshire Extension | CR | 24 | 15 |
| Leek & Manifold Valley Light | NSR | 13.3 | 8.25 |
| Maryport & Carlisle | | 110.9 | 68.9 |
| Mold & Denbigh Junction | LNWR | 24 | 15 |
| North & South Western Junction | LNWR | 13.6 | 5.25 |
| North London: | | | |
|   Owned | | 22.9 | 14.25 |
|   Share of joint lines | | 2.9 | 1.8 |
|   Total route | | 25.7 | 16 |
| Portpatrick & Wigtownshire Joint | LNWR, MR, CR, G & SWR | 131.9 | 82 |
| Shropshire Union Railways & Canal (Stafford–Wellington) | LNWR, GWR | 17.3 | 10.75 |
| Solway Junction | CR | 19.7 | 12.25 |
| Stratford-upon-Avon & Midland Junction | | 108.8 | 67.6 |
| Tottenham & Forest Gate | MR | 9.6 | 6 |
| Wick & Lybster Light | HR | 21.7 | 13.5 |

| Company | Worked by | km | miles |
|---|---|---|---|
| Wirral: | | | |
|   Owned | | 21.9 | 13.6 |
|   Share of joint lines | | 0.16 | 0.1 |
|   Total | | 22 | 13.7 |
| Yorkshire Dales | | | |
|   (Skipton–Grassington) | MR | 14.5 | 9 |

## Joint Railways

| A   Wholly in LMS: | Owned by | km | miles |
|---|---|---|---|
| Ashby & Nuneaton | LNWR, MR | 17.8 | 29.25 |
| Carlisle Citadel Station & Goods | CR, G & SWR, | | |
|   Traffic Joint Committees | LNWR, MR | | |
| Enderby | LNWR, MR | 4.4 | 2.75 |
| Furness & Midland | FR, MR | 15.7 | 9.75 |
| Glasgow, Barrhead & Kilmarnock | | | |
|   Joint | CR, G & SWR | 47.9 | 29.75 |
| Glasgow & Paisley | CR, G & SWR | 22.9 | 14.25 |
| Lancashire Union | LNWR, LYR | 20.5 | 12.75 |
| North Union | LNWR, LYR | 10.5 | 6.5 |
| Preston & Longridge | LNWR, LYR | 12.9 | 8 |
| Preston & Wyre | LNWR, LYR | 74 | 46 |
| Whitehaven, Cleator & Egremont | LNWR, FR | 56.3 | 35 |

## B   Joint with LNER:

| Company | km | miles |
|---|---|---|
| Axholme Joint | 44.7 | 27.75 |
| Cheshire Lines Committee | 228.5 | 142 |
| Dumbarton & Balloch | 11.27 | 7 |
| Dundee & Arbroath (including Carmyllie Light) | 37 | 23 |
| Great Central & Midland Joint | 64.8 | 40.25 |
| Great Central, Hull & Barnsley & Midland Joint | | |
|   ($\frac{1}{3}$ share) | 6.4 | 4 |
| Great Central & North Staffordshire Joint | 17.7 | 11 |
| Great Northern & LNWR Joint | 72.4 | 45 |

| Company | km | miles |
|---|---|---|
| Halifax & Ovenden | 4 | 2.5 |
| Halifax High Level | 4.8 | 3 |
| Manchester South Junction & Altrincham | 15.3 | 9.5 |
| Methley | 9.6 | 6 |
| Midland & Great Northern Joint | 295 | 183.25 |
| Norfolk & Suffolk Junction Committee | 35.8 | 22.25 |
| Oldham, Ashton & Guide Bridge | 10 | 6.25 |
| Ottley & Ilkley | 10 | 6.25 |
| Perth General Station Committee (⅓ share) | | |
| Princes Dock, Glasgow | 2 | 1.25 |
| South Yorkshire Joint (⅔ share) | 33 | 20.5 |
| Swinton & Knottingley Joint | 31.4 | 19.5 |
| Tottenham & Hampstead | 7.6 | 4.75 |
| **C** Joint with GWR: See GWR | | |
| **D** Joint with SR: Somerset & Dorset Joint | 169 | 105 |
| **E** Joint with GWR & SR: West London Extension | 8.4 | 2 |
| **F** Joint with Metropolitan District: Whitechapel & Bow | 3.2 | 2 |

## LMS Totals at 1 January 1923

| | km | miles |
|---|---|---|
| Owned | 11 294.4 | 7 018.2 |
| Lines leased or worked | 18.7 | 11.6 |
| Share of joint lines | 730 | 453.6 |
| Share of lines leased or worked jointly | 67.75 | 42.1 |
| TOTAL route | 12 110.6 | 7 525.4 |

*Rolling stock:*

| | |
|---|---|
| Tender locomotives | 6 916 |
| Tank locomotives | 3 376 |
| Departmental locomotives | 50 |
| TOTAL locomotives | 10 342 |
| Carriages, including electric stock | 27 229 |
| Wagons | 302 550 |
| Service vehicles | 22 933 |

## LONDON & NORTH EASTERN RAILWAY

| Company | Owned | Share of joint lines | Lines leased or worked | Share of lines leased or worked jointly | Total route |
|---|---|---|---|---|---|
| | km miles | km miles | km miles | km miles | km miles |
| North Eastern Railway[1] | 2 894.3 1 798.5 | 79.2 49.2 | 29.8 18.5 | | 3 003.1 1 866.1 |
| Great Northern Railway | 1 120.9 696.5 | 402.8 250.3 | 159 98.8 | 9 5.6 | 1 691.8 1 051.25 |
| Great Central Railway[2] | 1 015.6 631 | 143.5 89.2 | 96.7 60.1 | 120.4 74.8 | 1 376.1 855.1 |
| Great Eastern Railway | 1 637 1 017.2 | 120.4 74.8 | 13 8.1 | 1.1 0.7 | 1 916.5 1 190.9 |
| North British Railway | 2 055.2 1 277.1 | 26.4 16.4 | 128.6 79.9 | 6.8 4.25 | 2 217.2 1 377.7 |
| Great North of Scotland R | 538 334.3 | 0.3 0.2 | | | 538.3 334.5 |
| [1]North Eastern Railway included Hull & Barnsley R amalg. 1.4.1922 | 127 78.9 | 25.7 16 | 18.5 11.5 | | 171.2 106.4 |
| [2]Great Central Railway included Lancashire, Derbyshire & East Coast R amalg. 1.1.1907 | 93.7 58.25 | 2.4 1.5 | | | 96.1 59.75 |

## Subsidiary Companies

| Company | Worked by | km | miles |
|---|---|---|---|
| Brackenhill Light | NER | | |
| Colne Valley & Halstead | | 30.6 | 19 |

Crossover with timbers of Jarrah being installed at the new Severn Valley Railway station at Kidderminster, Worcestershire, on 23 July 1984. (John Marshall)

| Company | Worked by | km | miles |
|---|---|---|---|
| East & West Yorkshire Union | | 14.9 | 9.25 |
| East Lincolnshire (leased to GNR 1849) | | 76.4 | 47.5 |
| Edinburgh & Bathgate (leased to NBR 1869) | | 16.5 | 10.25 |
| Forcett | NER | 8.8 | 5.5 |
| Forth & Clyde Junction (leased to NBR 1875) | | 49 | 30.5 |
| Gifford & Garvald | NBR | 14.9 | 9.25 |
| Great North of England, Clarence & Hartlepool Junction (leased to NER) | | 10.9 | 6.75 |
| Horncastle (leased to GNR 1855) | | 12 | 7.5 |
| Humber Commercial Railway & Dock (leased to GCR) | | | |
| Kilsyth & Bonnybridge | CR + NBR | 13.7 | 8.5 |
| Lauder Light | NBR | 16.5 | 10.25 |
| London & Blackwall (leased to GER 1865) | | 9.6 | 6 |
| Mansfield (Kirkby Junction – Clipstone) | GCR | 16 | 10 |
| Mid-Suffolk Light | | 31.4 | 19.5 |

| Company | Worked by | km | miles |
|---|---|---|---|
| Newburgh & North Fife | NBR | 21.3 | 13.25 |
| North Lindsay Light | GCR | 19.3 | 12 |
| Nottingham & Grantham Railway & Canal (leased to GNR 1861) | | 37 | 23 |
| Nottingham Joint Station Committee | GNR + GCR | | |
| Nottingham Suburban | GNR | 6.4 | 4 |
| Seaforth & Sefton Junction (leased to GCR 1909) | Not built | | |
| Sheffield District | GCR (LD & ECR) | 8.8 | 5.5 |
| South Yorkshire Junction | NER (H & B) | 18.5 | 11.5 |
| Stamford & Essendine (leased to GNR 1894) | | 20.1 | 12.5 |
| West Riding Railway Committee (incorporated 1862 as West Riding & Grimsby). Vested in GNR & GCR 1867. Including Crofton branch, 1.6 km (1 mile) | | 52.3 | 32.5 |

## Joint Railways

| | | | |
|---|---|---|---|
| **A Wholly LNER:** | | | |
| GN & GE Joint | | 197.9 | 123 |
| West Riding & Grimsby (GN & GC) | | 50.7 | 31.5 |
| **B Joint with LMS: See LMS** | | | |
| **C Joint with GWR: See GWR** | | | |
| **D Other joint lines:** | | | |
| East London (with SR) | | 8 | 5 |
| Metropolitan & GC Joint | | 82.9 | 51.5 |

## Other Lines Worked

| | | | |
|---|---|---|---|
| Forth Bridge (NBR) | | 6.8 | 4.25 |
| Kings Lynn Railway & Docks (GER) | | 14.5 | 9 |

## LNER Totals at 1 January 1923

|  | km | miles |
|---|---|---|
| Owned | 10 150 | 6 307 |
| Share of joint lines | 481 | 298.9 |
| Lines leased or worked | 47 | 29.2 |
| Share of lines leased or worked jointly | 127.5 | 79.25 |
| TOTAL route | 10 805.3 | 6 714.3 |

*Rolling stock:*

| | |
|---|---|
| Tender locomotives | 4 746 |
| Tank locomotives | 2 639 |
| Electric locomotives | 13 |
| Departmental locomotives | 15 |
| TOTAL locomotives | 7 413 |
| Carriage stock | 21 348 |
| Wagons | 281 748 |
| Service vehicles | 17 635 |

Reproduction of an old Great Western Railway disc and crossbar signal at Didcot, Oxfordshire, on 27 May 1983. When the crossbar faced the train it indicated danger; when rotated through 90 degrees the disc indicated all clear. (John Marshall)

## SOUTHERN RAILWAY

| Company | Owned | Share of joint lines | Lines leased or worked | Share of lines leased or worked jointly | Total route |
|---|---|---|---|---|---|
| | km miles | km miles | km miles | km miles | km miles |
| London & South | 1 387.5 | 16 | 46.3 | 92.85 | 1 640.2 |
| Western | 862.2 | 10 | 28.8 | 57.7 | 1 019.2 |
| London, Brighton | 693.6 | 29.5 | 13.2 | 1.6 | 737.9 |
| & South Coast | 431 | 17.1 | 8.2 | 1 | 457.3 |
| South Eastern | 1 005.9 | 11.7 | 6.1 | 2.6 | 1 026.4 |
| & Chatham[1] | 625.1 | 7.3 | 3.8 | 1.6 | 637.8 |

[1] SE & C formed in 1899 as a working union of the South Eastern Railway and the London, Chatham & Dover Railway, maintaining separate accounts.

## Subsidiary Companies

| Company | Worked by | km | miles |
|---|---|---|---|
| Bridgwater | S & D Jt | 11.7 | 7.25 |
| Isle of Wight | | 22.9 | 14.25 |
| Isle of Wight Central | | 46 | 28.6 |
| North Cornwall | LSWR | 80.5 | 50 |
| Plymouth & Dartmoor (1372 mm (4 ft 6 in) gauge) | LSWR | 3.6 | 2.25 |
| Plymouth, Devonport & South Western Junction | | 35.4 | 22 |
| Sidmouth | LSWR | 13.2 | 8.25 |
| Hayling | LBSCR | 8 | 5 |
| London & Greenwich | SER | 6 | 3.75 |
| Mid Kent (Bromley–St Mary Cray) | LC & DR | 4 | 2.5 |
| Victoria Station & Pimlico | GWR, LNWR, LC & DR | 2 | 1.25 |

| Company | Worked by | km | miles |
|---|---|---|---|
| Brighton & Dyke | LBSCR | 7.6 | 4.75 |
| Freshwater, Yarmouth & Newport (IOW) | | 19.3 | 12 |
| Lee-on-Solent | LSWR | 4.8 | 3 |

**Joint Railways**

| A   Wholly in SR: | Owned by | km | miles |
|---|---|---|---|
| Croydon & Oxted | LBSCR + SER | 20.1 | 12.5 |
| Dover & Deal | SER + LCDR | 13.7 | 8.5 |
| Epsom & Leatherhead | LBSCR + LSWR | 6 | 3.75 |
| Portsmouth & Ryde (Cosham–Portsmouth Harbour, Ryde Pier) | LSWR + LBSCR | 13.7 | 8.5 |
| Tooting, Merton & Wimbledon | LSWR + LBSCR | 9.25 | 5.75 |
| Woodside & South Croydon | LBSCR/SE & C (alternate years) | 4 | 2.5 |

Prototype British Railways Advanced Passenger Train trailer unit 370001 at Carnforth in July 1978 during trials, showing the driving end and nose module. (John Marshall)

**B    Joint with Other Railways:**

| Company | km | miles |
|---|---|---|
| East London, with LNER, Met, Met District | 8 | 5 |
| Easton & Church Hope, with GWR | 5.6 | 3.5 |
| Somerset & Dorset Joint, with LMS | 169 | 105 |
| West London Extension, with GWR, LMS | 7.6 | 4.75 |
| Weymouth & Portland, with GWR | 8.8 | 5.5 |

## Southern Railway Totals at 1 January 1923

| | km | miles |
|---|---|---|
| Owned | 3 433.9 | 2 133.8 |
| Share of joint lines | 81.1 | 50.4 |
| Lines leased or worked | 12.7 | 7.9 |
| Share of lines leased or worked jointly | 11.1 | 6.9 |
| TOTAL route | 3 522.75 | 2 189 |

*Rolling stock:*

| | |
|---|---|
| Tender locomotives | 1 180 |
| Tank locomotives | 1 078 |
| Departmental locomotives | 6 |
| TOTAL locomotives | 2 264 |
| Carriage stock | 1 073 |
| Wagons | 35 905 |
| Service vehicles | 2 522 |

## NATIONALISATION OF BRITISH RAILWAYS

Proposals for nationalisation of British railways date back to Gladstone's Railway Bill of 1844 which provided for state ownership of all railways authorised after 1844. The proposals did not reach the Act, but nationalisation was proposed on several subsequent occasions and was discussed at length in Parliament in May 1873.

As during World War I, the railways were again taken over by the British

Government in World War II and were used almost beyond the limits of their capacity. In 1945 the Attlee Government decided on a programme of nationalisation and under the Transport Act, 6 August 1947 Ch 49, the British Transport Commission was set up and all the main-line railways, a number of dock, canal and inland navigation and road haulage undertakings were transferred to it.

The railways nationalised from 1 January 1948 were:

| Company | km | miles |
|---|---|---|
| GWR | 6 085.5 | 3 781.5 |
| LMS | 11 015.6 | 6 845 |
| LNER | 10 215.8 | 6 349 |
| SR | 3 469.6 | 2 156 |
| London Passenger Transport Board | 280 | 174 |
| TOTAL | 31 066.5 | 19 305.5 |

## British Railways Rolling Stock at 1 January 1948

| Company | Steam locos | Electric locos | Electric power cars | Passenger train vehicles | Freight vehicles | Service and misc. vehicles |
|---|---|---|---|---|---|---|
| GWR | 3 631 | | | 8 697 | 82 453 | 9 545 |
| LMS | 7 644 | | 268 | 23 541 | 286 611 | 14 508 |
| LNER | 6 518 | 13 | 193 | 19 626 | 258 236 | 11 732 |
| SR | 1 819 | | 3 032 | 5 413 | 33 709 | 1 698 |
| LPTB | 14 | 47 | 1 749 | 1 954 | | 450 |
| TOTALS | 19 626 | 60 | 5 242 | 64 280 | 660 009 | 37 933 |

The railways were divided into five regions: Scottish, North Eastern, London Midland, Eastern, Western and Southern. The Eastern and North Eastern regions were combined on 1 January 1967.

Under the Transport Act of 1 August 1962 the British Transport Commission was dissolved and the British Railways Board was set up to manage the railways, and the London Transport Board to manage the London Underground railways and the buses. The BRB operated from 1 January 1963.

Under the Transport Act of 25 October 1968 the regional structure was abolished but was continued by the BRB from 1 January 1969 as part of its management structure. The National Freight Corporation was set up to provide integrated road and rail freight services. Freightliners Ltd, owned 51 per cent by the NFC and 49 per cent by the BRB, was formed to develop the freightliner services.

Under the Transport (London) Act 1969 the London Transport Board was de-nationalised and was transferred to Greater London Council as the London Transport Executive. On 29 June 1984, under the London Regional Transport Act of 26 June, it was re-nationalised and renamed London Regional Transport.

British Rail Engineering Ltd was formed on 1 January 1970 as a wholly-owned subsidiary of the BRB to control the former railway workshops, with facilities to take on outside contracts.

Local Government Acts in 1972 and 1974 gave local authorities responsibilities for passenger transport in their areas. They work with BR to plan and finance passenger services.

During the 1960s, under the guidance of Dr Richard Beeching, British Railways route length was reduced from 30 209 km (18 771 miles) in 1960 to 21 342 km (13 261 miles) in 1969. By the end of 1982 it had come down to 17 229 km (10 706 miles).

## British Railway Route Length, 1830–1980

| | km | miles | | km | miles |
|---|---|---|---|---|---|
| 1830 | c 190 | c 120 | 1910 | 32 152 | 19 997 |
| 1840 | 2 388 | 1 484 | 1920 | 32 710 | 20 326 |
| 1850 | 9 790 | 6 084 | 1930 | 32 902 | 20 445[1] |
| 1860 | 14 594 | 9 069 | 1940 | 32 551 | 20 227 |
| 1870 | 21 826 | 13 563 | 1950 | 31 848 | 19 790 |
| 1880 | 25 035 | 15 557 | 1960 | 30 208 | 18 771 |
| 1890 | 27 799 | 17 274 | 1970 | 18 988 | 11 799 |
| 1900 | 30 037 | 18 665 | 1980 | 17 641 | 10 961 |

[1] British Railways reached their maximum total route length in 1931: 32 908 km (20 449 miles).

## Standard-gauge Route Open for Traffic at End of 1982

|                       | km     | miles  |
|-----------------------|--------|--------|
| Passenger traffic only | 1 160  | 721    |
| Passenger and freight  | 13 210 | 8 029  |
| Freight only           | 2 858  | 1 776  |
| TOTAL route            | 17 229 | 10 706 |

## Length of Track Open for Traffic at End of 1982

|                                              | km      | miles  |
|----------------------------------------------|---------|--------|
| Running lines                                | 34 287  | 21 306 |
| Sidings                                      | 7 055   | 4 384  |
| TOTAL track                                  | 41 342  | 25 690 |
| Length of electrified track:                 |         |        |
| Running lines, AC overhead 25 kV 50 Hz       | 5 029   | 3 125  |
| DC overhead 1 500 V                          | 67.5    | 42     |
| DC 3rd rail 600–750 V[1]                     | 4 165   | 2 588  |
| Sidings, all systems                         | 668     | 415    |
| TOTAL electrified track                      | 9 929.5 | 6 190  |
| Route electrified: AC overhead               | 1 937   | 1 204  |
| DC overhead                                  | 27[2]   | 17[2]  |
| DC third rail                                | 1 788   | 1 111  |
| TOTAL electrified                            | 3 752   | 2 332  |

[1] Manchester–Bury, 16 km (10 miles), 1200 V.
[2] Manchester–Hadfield–Glossop. Being converted to 25 kV 50 Hz 1983–4. Also owned by BR: Vale of Rheidol branch, 600 mm (1 ft 11½ in) gauge, 19 km (11.8 miles).

## British Railways Track

Since 1966 the standard BR track gauge has been 1432 mm (4 ft 8⅜ in), using vertical rails. The gauge was narrowed by 3 mm to reduce the tendency of bogies to 'hunt' (veer from side to side) at high speeds. Earlier track still in use has a gauge of 1435 mm (4 ft 8½ in) with rails inclined inwards at 1 in 20.

The standard British rail weighs 56.1 kg/m (113 lb/yd). Rails are made in lengths of 18.29 m (60 ft) and are welded at depots into lengths of 183–275 m (600–900 ft).

Sleepers for plain line are of concrete, hardwood (Jarrah) and softwood. Pre-stressed concrete sleepers are used with continuous welded rail; they measure 2515 mm (8 ft 3 in) long and weigh 267 kg (588 lb). They are now cheaper than wooden sleepers and are expected to have a useful life of over 50 years. Softwood sleepers measure 254 × 127 mm (10 × 5 in) in section and are 2591 mm (8 ft 6 in) long. Their life varies from 12 to 25 years, and they are now little used. Jarrah sleepers, measuring 254 × 120 mm (10 × 4¾ in) can last from 30 to 40 years.

Under switches and crossings they are known as 'timbers' and here they measure 305 × 152 mm (12 × 6 in). Experiments are being made with concrete bearers under switches and crossings. They are satisfactory in standard layouts where they can be cast with holes for bolts.

The standard rail fastening is the Pandrol Rail Clip, by far the simplest and most effective rail fastening yet devised. The principal component is a spring-steel clip quickly driven into place with a hammer and as easily removed. Its resilience makes it unaffected by vibration, it will not work loose, and it prevents 'rail creep' (the tendency for rails to move in the direction of the traffic when a train is braking). Concrete sleepers are cast complete with Pandrol housings.

Insertion and extraction of Pandrol clips have now been mechanised to reduce line-occupation periods. The 'Pandriver' travels along the track at about 0.75 km/h (0.5 mph), enabling a man to place clips in position ahead of the machine. The 'Pandrex' knocks out clips at a track speed of 3 km/h (2 mph).

At changes from straight to curved track, or between curves of different radii, transition curves are necessary to enable a train to negotiate the change safely at high speed.

On curves the track is canted; that is, the outer rail is raised to tilt the train inwards to balance centrifugal forces as the train rounds the curve. The amount of cant is an optimum below that theoretically required for the highest speed, and does not exceed 150 mm (6 in). Cant is built up and reduced gradually in transition curves.

The formation beneath the track consists of a bed of ballast 300–400 mm (12–16 in) deep. The ballast provides drainage, spreads the load over the ground beneath and provides lateral stability to the track. This is particularly necessary with continuous welded rail for which the ballast shoulders, or the amount beyond the ends of the sleepers, is increased to resist a tendency to buckle in hot weather. Expansive forces are contained as compressive stresses within the rail. Crushed rock forms the best ballast. Limestone was formerly used but recently other hard rocks such as granite are more frequently used. Shingle and pebbles are useless as ballast, except on the lightest tracks, because of the ease with which the stones slide one against the other.

The ballast also permits track alignment vertically and horizontally by mechanical or hand tamping and fettling. Where the track foundation is clay it is now the practice to lay polythene sheeting over it to prevent it working up into the ballast when wet.

Experiments have been made with Paved Concrete Track (PACT). This consists of a continuous slab of concrete to which the rail fastenings are attached. Its advantage is that it needs almost no maintenance. Disadvantages are high first cost, the length of line-occupation time during installation and, if PACT is used over more than short distances, the necessity to alter train lavatories so that they do not deposit waste onto the track. So its use in Britain has been confined to tunnels and between retaining walls in cuttings, where access for maintenance is difficult or dangerous.

For relaying, track is made up in jigs in 18.29 m (60 ft) long panels which are taken to the relaying site and lowered onto a prepared bed. Ballast is tipped into position and fettled and the track lined up. About a week later the 60 ft rails are removed and replaced by continuous welded rails. Slewing jacks are used on curves and the correct radius is established by measuring the versine, or offset, from the centre of a chord. The radius of a curve can be established by the formula $R = 125L^2/V$ where $R$ = radius in metres, $L$ = length of chord in metres, $V$ = versine in millimetres. Radius in feet is given by the formula $R = 3L^2/2V$ where $L$ is the length of the chord in feet and $V$ is the versine in inches.

## Locomotives and Rolling Stock

| *British Railways rolling stock at the end of 1983:* | |
| --- | ---: |
| Diesel locomotives | 2 603 |
| Electric locomotives | 247 |
| Steam locomotives (600 mm gauge) | 3 |
| TOTAL locomotives | 2 853 |
| Advanced Passenger Train (APT) power cars | 6 |
| APT passenger carriages | 30 |
| High Speed Train (HST) power cars | 197 |
| HST passenger carriages | 709 |

*Coaching stock:*

| | |
|---|---:|
| Passenger carriages, loco hauled | 4 059 |
| Diesel multiple-unit power cars and trailers | 2 703 |
| Electric multiple-unit power cars and trailers | 7 306 |
| Coaching stock vehicles, 600 mm gauge | 17 |
| TOTAL passenger carriages | 14 085 |
| Non-passenger carrying vehicles | 2 156 |
| TOTAL coaching stock | 16 241 |
| TOTAL seats or berths in passenger carriages | 971 097 |

*Freight vehicles:*

| | |
|---|---:|
| Covered | 2 518 |
| Open | 42 673 |
| Flat | 7 916 |
| Bulk material | 1 403 |
| TOTAL | 54 510 |
| Containers | 15 |
| TOTAL capacity of freight vehicles | 1 488 061 tonnes |

## Passenger and Freight Traffic

| | 1938 | 1951 | 1963 | 1982 |
|---|---:|---:|---:|---:|
| Passenger stations | 6 698 | 6 214 | 4 306 | 2 369 |
| Passenger journeys, 000s | 1 205 586 | 1 001 308 | 921 514 | 718 488 |
| Freight stations | 6 908 | 6 512 | 5 165 | 339 |
| Marshalling yards | | 958 | 602 | 59 |
| Coal and coke carried, 000 tons | 168 852 | 169 388 | 151 029 | 88 400 |
| Total freight, 000 tons | 263 665 | 284 803 | 234 865 | 141 900 |
| Freight ton-miles, millions | 16 672 | 22 902 | 16 537 | 10 877 |
| Railway horses | 12 742 | 3 294 | Last one 1967 | |

## British Rail Fares

British rail passenger fares, although among the highest in the world in relation to average earned income, have roughly kept pace with incomes. As an example, the standard return fare for the 304 km (188¾ miles) from London to Manchester (third class until 1956, then second class) increased as follows in 30 years:

|      | £     | Approximate value in 1982 |
|------|-------|---------------------------|
| 1952 | 2.68  | 20.00                     |
| 1962 | 4.25  | 24.00                     |
| 1972 | 7.55  | 26.00                     |
| 1982 | 35.00 | 35.00                     |

On the same basis a person, for example a teacher, earning £500 a year in 1952 should have earned £500 × 35 ÷ 2.68 = £6529.85 in 1982, which is about correct. Thus the fare represents about 1.4 days earnings for a person in this category.

## Staff Employed by British Rail

| 1938    | 1951    | 1967    | 1972    | 1982    |
|---------|---------|---------|---------|---------|
| 581 401 | 599 890 | 279 371 | 229 636 | 161 407 |

British Railways efficiency in terms of train-km per member of staff increased by 79.5 per cent from 1955 to 1978, but that of the Netherlands Railways increased by 93.2 per cent. Italian Railways in the same period showed a fall of 13.4 per cent. In 1978 BR operated 2525 train-km per member of staff, roughly equal to Switzerland with 2581. Netherlands Railways operated 4131, the highest in the EEC. The lowest were Austria, 1347, and Italy 1367.

British Rail is endeavouring to increase its manpower efficiency by flexible rostering of train crews, single manning of traction units, elimination of guards on many passenger and freight trains, and 'open' stations, but progress is impeded by trade unions because of fear of unemployment.

The result of a rigid 8-hour shift for footplate staff is that each man spends an average of 3 h 58 min driving. Men engaged on passenger trains drive an average of about 29 000 loaded train-km (18 000 train-miles) in a year, about twice the annual mileage of an average motorist.

The abbreviated title 'British Rail' and its new totem, two horizontal lines and two arrow heads, were adopted in the summer of 1964. The totem began to appear on rolling stock in February 1965.

The first BR combined timetable, including all regions in one volume, replacing the separate regional timetables, operated from 6 May 1974 to 4 May 1975. It had 1345 pages $254 \times 190$ mm ($10 \times 7\frac{1}{2}$ in) and cost 50p. The reduced size timetable, 1160 pages, $210 \times 144$ mm ($8\frac{1}{4} \times 5\frac{3}{4}$ in), appeared in 1982, price 'only £2.90'.

British Railways only steam-operated line, the 600 mm (1 ft 11⅝ in) gauge Vale of Rheidol Railway in Wales. A train at the upper terminus at Devil's Bridge on 30 July 1963 headed by 2-6-2 tank No 7 *Owain Glyndwr*. (John Marshall)

## **LONDON TRANSPORT**

London Regional Transport operates services over a total route length of 410 km (255 miles) of which 383 km (238 miles) are administered by LT, the remainder by British Rail. A total of 159 km (99 miles) are underground of which 124 km (77 miles) are in small-diameter deep-level tube tunnels and 35 km (22 miles) are in sub-surface, mostly 'cut and cover' tunnels. The greatest depth below the surface is 67.3 m (221 ft) below Hampstead Heath, 579 m (633 yd) north of Hampstead station on the Northern Line. There are 279 stations of which 250 are managed by LT. Ventilation is provided by 93 fans handling nearly 2400 m³ (84 756 ft³) of air per second, excluding the Victoria Line which has 16 fans handling 531 m³ (18 752 ft³) per second. At 31 stations on the older system and at all stations on the Victoria Line draught relief shafts are provided to cope with the air moved by the trains. LT owns 2843 motor cars, 1380 trailer cars and 330 other vehicles. Electric supply is by third rail at 600 V dc outside the running rails and an insulated fourth rail in the centre as return conductor. In 1981 the system carried about 539 million passengers.

Of 1 250 000 journeys to work in Central London, LT carries 34 per cent by underground railway and 14 per cent by bus. BR carries 460 000, or nearly 40 per cent, and two thirds of this on Southern Region.

The various sections of London Transport railways were first opened, and completed, as follows:

Metropolitan:

first section, Paddington–Farringdon, 10 January 1863

last section, to Verney Junction, 1 April 1894

District Railway:

first section, South Kensington–Westminster, 24 December 1868

last section, Whitechapel–Upminster, 2 June 1902

Northern Line:

first section, City & South London, Stockwell–King William Street, 18 December 1890

last section, to Mill Hill East on former GNR Edgware line, 18 May 1941

Central Line:

first section, Shepherds Bush–Bank, 30 July 1900

last section, Epping–Ongar (former GER) 25 September 1949

Piccadilly Line:

first section, Hammersmith–Finsbury Park, 15 December 1906

last section, to Heathrow Central, 16 December 1977

Bakerloo Line:

first section, Baker Street–Waterloo, 10 March 1906

last section, Baker Street—Wembley Park, 20 November 1939 (and Stanmore 10 December 1932) now Jubilee Line

Victoria Line:

first section, Walthamstow—Warren Street, 1 December 1968

last section, to Brixton 23 July 1971

Jubilee Line:

first section, Kingsbury—Stanmore (formerly Bakerloo Line), 10 December 1932

last section, Baker Street—Charing Cross, 1 May 1979

The Central Line carries the greatest number of passengers over one track, 28 000 in one hour. The most frequent service is on the southbound Bakerloo Line between Baker Street and Waterloo at the morning peak; 33 trains in 1 hour, 18 in one peak $\frac{1}{2}$ hour.

The first LT train with automatic driving equipment entered experimental service on the District Line on 8 April 1963. Full-scale trials on the 6.5 km (4 mile) Woodford—Hinault shuttle service on the Central Line began on 5 April 1964. The entire service on the Victoria Line is operated by automatic trains.

The deepest lift shaft on the London Underground is at Hampstead station, 55 m (181 ft) deep. The lift operates at a maximum speed of 243.8 m (800 ft) a minute. Hampstead is the deepest station on LT, 58.5 m (192 ft) below ground.

The longest escalator on the London Underground is that serving the Piccadilly Line at Leicester Square station. The shaft is 49.3 m (161 ft 6 in) long with a vertical rise of 24.6 m (80 ft 9 in).

# 5 French Railways

Société Nationale des Chemins de fer Français (SNCF)
French National Railways Company.

The first public railway in France, from Saint-Etienne to Andrézieux, was begun in 1824 and formally opened on 1 October 1828. The Concession had been granted on 26 February 1823. The railway worked unofficially from May 1827. Passenger traffic began on 1 March 1832, but horse-traction was used until 1 August 1844. The track consisted of cast-iron fish-bellied rails. It was extended from Saint-Etienne to the Loire in 1828 with wrought-iron rails. On 7 June 1826 a Concession was granted for the Saint-Etienne–Lyon Railway and the section from Givors to Rive-de-Gier was opened on 25 June 1830. The remainder of the railway from Lyon to Givors was opened on 3 April 1832 and from the Rive-de-Gier to Saint-Etienne for goods on 18 October 1832 and passengers on 25 February 1833.

At the end of 1937 the principal railways of France consisted of the following systems: Est; Nord; Paris, Lyon & Mediterranean (PLM); Paris–Orleans; Midi (Southern); State; and Alsace-Lorraine. From 1 January 1938 these were amalgamated into one system, the SNCF or French National Railways Company, formed under a decree of 31 August 1937. Under the decree the original companies continued as financial entities until 1955, the average date of expiry of their various concessions.

The system was divided into six regions: Northern; Eastern; South-Eastern; Mediterranean; South Western; and Western. On 1 January 1972 the Eastern, South-Eastern and Mediterranean Regions were reduced to two known as Réseau de l'Est and Réseau du Sud-Est, or Eastern Network and South-Eastern Network, sub-divided into 12 Regions. On 1 January 1973 the Northern, Western and South-Western Regions were made into three Réseaux sub-divided into 13 Regions. So SNCF now consists of five Réseaux, or Networks, divided into 25 Regions. Under the decree of 1937 the SNCF had power to operate the railways until 31 December 1982. During 1982 the legal status of the SNCF was completely reviewed and was re-established by a new decree on 18 February 1983. The financial structure was to be overhauled and modifications were to be made in the executive council. The role of the SNCF as a public service was re-affirmed, with emphasis on constant improvement of standards, and the attraction of new customers. New arrangements with the State were to be made with a view towards future financial solvency. On 1 January 1983 the SNCF took over operation of the Corsican Railways.

## Railway Development in France

| Year | km | miles | Year | km | miles |
|------|------|------|------|------|------|
| 1840 | 410 | 255 | 1920 | 41 599 | 25 849 |
| 1850 | 2 659 | 1 852 | 1930 | 42 199 | 26 222 |
| 1860 | 9 410 | 5 847 | 1940 | 39 999 | 24 855 |
| 1870 | 17 400 | 10 812 | 1950 | 41 299 | 25 663 |
| 1880 | 23 599 | 14 664 | 1960 | 38 857 | 24 145 |
| 1890 | 32 899 | 20 443 | 1972 | 35 180 | 21 860 |
| 1900 | 36 798 | 22 866 | 1982 | 34 362 | 21 352 |
| 1910 | 38 898 | 24 171 | | | |

By the end of 1982 22 500 km (13 981 miles) of route were laid with continuous welded rail.

## Electrification

Of the total route length of 34 362 km (21 352 miles) a total of 10 074 km (6260 miles) is electrified representing 29.3 per cent of the system, as follows:

| | km | miles |
|------|------|------|
| 25 kV 50 Hz | 4 497 | 2 794 |
| 1500 V dc overhead | 5 462 | 3 394 |
| 850 V dc 3rd rail | 63 | 39 |
| 750 V dc 3rd rail | 18 | 11 |
| 600 V dc 3rd rail | 34 | 21 |

## TGV Services

Trains à Grande Vitesse (TGVs) or High Speed Trains are electric train sets consisting of eight coaches with a power unit, or locomotive, at each end.

The coaches are articulated as one unit on nine bogies. The power units are each mounted on two four-wheeled bogies and altogether six bogies are motored, a total of 12 motors normally working at 1070 V, 530 A, but capable of withstanding 1000 A for up to 7 minutes without overheating. The motors are body-mounted to reduce unsprung weight. Rheostatic braking on motor bogies supplements electro-pneumatic disc brakes. Clasp brakes are also fitted, but these work only below 200 km/h (124 mph). The trains are designed to run on both 25 kV 50 Hz and 1500 V dc, and a third type is planned, also on 15 kV 16⅔ Hz, for working through into Switzerland. Thyristors regulate voltage at motor terminals, operating as a mixed bridge on 25 kV ac and as a chopper on 1500 V dc. On 25 kV they have a continuous power rating of 6450 kW, on 1500 V dc of 3100 kW, and on 15 kV of 2800 kW. Each set has a tare weight of 386 tonnes (first class only units 384 tonnes) and a total length of 200.19 m (656 ft 9 in) over couplings. Power units are 22.15 m (72 ft 8 in) long. The trains have seats for 111 first class and 275 second class passengers (first class only trains seat 287).

On 26 February 1981 TGV set No 23016 attained a top speed of 380 km/h (236 mph) near Tonnerre in central France during a test run. On 27 September 1981 TGVs began a regular hourly service between Paris and Lyons, covering the 426 km (265 miles) in 2 h 40 min, to be reduced later to 2 h. Maximum speed is 260 km/h (162 mph) and speeds up to 300 km/h (186 mph) are planned. As further stock became available services were extended to the Rhône Valley and Midi areas in early summer 1982 with four daily return trips between Paris and Marseilles and three between Paris and Montpellier, increased in September to eight and four respectively.

The reliability of the TGVs has been proved by an average failure rate of only one in 1 428 571 train-km (887 671 train-miles). At the end of 1982 there were 57 train sets in operation. A total of 87 sets is planned, to include 75 dual-voltage 1st and 2nd class, six first class only and six triple-voltage first and second class units. They are being built by Alsthorn-Atlantique of Belfort and Francorail MTE.

This reliability has induced the French Post Office to order two eight-car and one four-car postal TGV sets to carry mail between Paris and the south and east of France. These would consume only one sixth of the energy used by aircraft doing the same work. A ten-car unit is planned to carry 75 tonnes of mail in 250 containers, five times the capacity of one aircraft.

Track for the TGV sets consists of rails of 60 kg/m (121 lb/yd) inclined inwards at 1 in 20. Sleepers are of the tied twin-block type 2.4 m (7 ft 10 in) long, weighing 245 kg (539 lb), at 600 mm (1 ft 11½ in) between centres. Ballast is 320 mm (12½ in) deep beneath the sleepers.

## Motive Power and Rolling Stock

|  | 1982 | 1972 | Percentage variation |
|---|---|---|---|
| Electric locomotives | 2 425 | 2 181 | +11 |
| Diesel locomotives | 2 126 | 2 102 | +1.1 |
| Electric motor coaches | 594 | 652 | −8.9 |
| Diesel railcars | 840 | 972 | −14 |
| Turbotrain sets | 53 | 13 | |
| TGV sets | 57 | | |

## Passenger Rolling Stock

|  | 1982 | 1972 | Percentage variation |
|---|---|---|---|
| Coaches | 11 216 | 11 689 | −4 |
| Other passenger vehicles | 4 524 | 3 831 | +18 |
| Average passenger-km per vehicle in service (millions) | 3.61 | 2.79 | +29 |

## Goods Rolling Stock

|  | 1982 | 1972 | Percentage variation |
|---|---|---|---|
| Bogie wagons | 113 500 | 73 900 | +54 |
| Other wagons | 135 300 | 228 700 | −40.8 |
| TOTAL wagons | 248 800 | 302 600 | −18 |
| Average number of wagons in service in France | 224 400 | 254 500 | −12 |
| Tonne-km per wagon in service | 273 000 | 270 000 | +1.1 |

Chapelon rebuilt compound 4–6–2 of the former Northern Railway of France.
(SNCF/French Railways Ltd)

## Usage and Performance of Various Forms of Motive Power

Distances travelled (thousands of km)

|  | 1982 | 1972 | Percentage variation |
|---|---|---|---|
| Electric locomotives | 342 700 | 307 100 | +12 |
| Diesel locomotives | 134 500 | 146 800 | −8.4 |
| Electric motor coaches | 61 100 | 61 300 | −0.3 |
| Diesel railcars | 83 900 | 92 000 | −8.8 |
| Turbotrain sets | 12 000 | 3 600 | |
| TGV sets | 15 500 | | |
| Maximum axle load: Motive power 23 tonnes | | | |
| Rolling stock 18–20 tonnes | | | |

French TGV (Train à Grande Vitesse) on the Paris–Lyons run on which speeds of
260 km/h (162 mph) are reached. (SNCF/French Railways–Lafontant)

## Revenue, tonne-km (millions)

|  | 1982 | 1972 | Percentage variation |
|---|---|---|---|
| Electric traction | 207 000 | 196 300 | + 5.5 |
| Diesel traction and turbotrains | 50 600 | 57 900 | − 13 |
| TOTAL | 257 600 | 254 500 | + 1.2 |
| Passenger trains | 104 100 | 83 500 | + 25 |
| Parcels trains | 45 300 | 37 800 | + 20 |
| Goods trains | 108 200 | 133 200 | − 19 |
| Revenue tonne-km by electric traction as percentage of total | 80.3 | 71.1 | |
| Average gross load per train in tonnes: | | | |
|   Parcels | 544 | 530 | + 2.6 |
|   Goods | 968 | 924 | + 4.8 |

## Energy Consumption

|  | 1982 | 1972 | Percentage variation |
|---|---|---|---|
| Electricity, millions of kWh | 5 863 | 5 581 | + 5.1 |
| Diesel fuel, thousands of m³ | 551 | 618 | − 11 |
|     thousands of gallons | 121 220 | 135 960 | |
| Various petroleum products | | | |
|   thousands of m³ | 70 | 196 | − 64 |
|   thousands of gallons | 15 400 | 43 120 | |
| Coal, coke, thousands of tonnes | 19.6 | 64.7 | − 70 |
| Total equivalent in oil, thousands of tonnes | 2 012 | 2 123 | − 5.2 |
| Energy consumption for traction: | | | |
| Electricity, millions of kWh | 5 312 | 5 046 | + 5.3 |
| Diesel fuel, thousands of m³ | 505 | 542 | − 6·8 |
|     thousands of gallons | 111 100 | 119 240 | |
| TOTAL equivalent in oil, thousands of tonnes | 1 713 | 1 619 | + 1.4 |

FRENCH RAILWAYS

**Passenger Traffic**

|  | 1982 | 1972 | Percentage variation |
|---|---|---|---|
| Passengers carried, millions | 270 | 225 | +20 |
| Passenger-km, millions | 49 180 | 36 510 | +35 |
| Average passenger journey, km | 182 | 162 | +12 |
| Train-km, millions: |  |  |  |
| 'Rapide' and Express trains | 166 | 131 | +27 |
| TGV | 8.8 |  |  |
| Local trains | 77.7 | 74.5 | +4.3 |
| Paris suburban: |  |  |  |
| Passengers carried, millions | 444 | 381 | +16.5 |
| Passenger-km, millions | 7 670 | 6 340 | +20.9 |
| Average passenger journey, km | 17.3 | 16.6 | +4.2 |
| Train-km, millions | 44.3 | 32.4 | +36.7 |
| TOTAL traffic |  |  |  |
| Passengers carried, millions | 714 | 606 | +18 |
| Passenger-km, millions | 56 850 | 42 850 | +33 |
| Average passenger journey, km | 79.6 | 71.0 | +12.1 |

**Goods Traffic**

|  | 1982 | 1972 | Percentage variation |
|---|---|---|---|
| Goods carried by rail wagons: |  |  |  |
| millions of tonnes | 181 | 243 | −26 |
| Tonne-km, millions | 59 620 | 67 190 | −11 |
| Goods carried by road, |  |  |  |
| millions of tonnes | 1.21 | 0.99 | +22 |
| Tonne-km, millions | 0.64 | 0.51 | +25 |
| TOTAL transported, millions of tonnes | 182 | 244 | −25 |
| TOTAL tonne-km, millions | 60 260 | 67 690 | −11 |

## Goods Transport by Consignments

|  | 1982 | 1972 | Percentage variation |
|---|---|---|---|
| *Millions of tonnes carried:* |  |  |  |
| National Express Parcels Service (SERNAM) | 1.81 | 1.45 | +24.8 |
| TOTAL | 2.02 | 1.99 | +1.5 |

## Total Goods Traffic

|  | 1982 | 1972 | Percentage variation |
|---|---|---|---|
| Millions of tonnes carried | 184 | 246 | −25 |
| Tonne-km, millions | 61 200 | 68 610 | −11 |
| Average wagon load of commercial (not SNCF) traffic, tonnes | 32.1 | 27 | +19 |
| Average distance per tonne, km | 332 | 278 | +19 |
| Train-km, millions: parcels | 83.2 | 71.3 | +17 |
| goods | 110.3 | 143.7 | −23 |

## Classified Goods, Millions of Tonne-km

|  | 1982 | 1972 | Percentage variation |
|---|---|---|---|
| Cereals, grain, vegetables, animal food | 4 830 | 3 630 | +33 |
| Perishable commodities | 2 100 | 3 790 | −45 |
| Dried grocery goods | 1 330 | 1 070 | +24 |
| Drinks | 3 720 | 3 570 | +4.2 |
| Solid fuel | 3 340 | 3 900 | −14 |
| Iron ore, minerals | 3 060 | 5 350 | −43 |
| Iron and steel products | 6 660 | 8 020 | −17 |

|  | 1982 | 1972 | Percentage variation |
|---|---|---|---|
| Electrical and mechanical appliances | 810 | 840 | −3.6 |
| Vehicles, agricultural machinery etc. | 1 980 | 1 810 | +9.4 |
| Petroleum products | 3 930 | 5 240 | −25 |
| Chemical, radio-active and explosive products | 4 210 | 3 910 | +7.7 |
| Fertilisers and manure | 4 440 | 5 960 | −26 |
| Stone and construction material | 5 820 | 8 390 | −31 |
| Timber, tanning extracts | 940 | 1 190 | −21 |
| Paper and packing materials | 1 010 | 1 240 | −19 |
| Containers | 3 690 ⎫ |  |  |
| Road vehicles on wagons (piggyback) | 2 420 ⎬ | 6 320 | +37 |
| All other kinds of goods | 2 540 ⎭ |  |  |
| TOTAL | 56 830 | 64 230 | −12 |

## Quality of Service

|  | 1982 | 1972 |
|---|---|---|
| Percentage of 'Rapide' and express trains arriving 15 or more minutes late | 3.5 | 4.5 |
| TGVs | 2.4 | — |
| Traction failures, per million train-km |  |  |
|   Electric locomotives | 4.6 | 6.4 |
|   Diesel locomotives | 11.6 | 14.8 |
|   Electric railcars | 8.2 | 7.1 |
|   Diesel railcars | 5.4 ⎫ | 7.3 |
|   Turbotrains | 4.5 ⎭ | |
|   TGVs | 0.7 | — |
| Catenary failures per 1000 km of electrified track | 87 | 91 |

## Permanent Way Work Carried Out, Thousands of km of Track

|  | 1982 | 1972 |
|---|---|---|
| Periodical servicing | 16 | 9.4 |
| Levelling, periodical or not | 14.9 | 16.4 |
| Complete renewal of track and ballast | 0.89 | 0.95 |
| Renewal of rails only | 0.17 | 0.1 |
| Renewal of ballast only | 0.08 | 0.08 |
| New rails used, thousands of tonnes | 125 | 150 |
| No of new sleepers, millions: wood | 0.94 | 2.20 |
| reinforced concrete | 1.58 | 0.69 |

## Numbers of Persons Employed in Various Departments

|  | 1982 | 1972 | Percentage variation |
|---|---|---|---|
| General management of system and networks | 7 340 |  |  |
| Administration at national level | 10 930 |  |  |
| Auxiliary services | 1 370 |  |  |
| Regional management | 11 950 |  |  |
| Administration at regional level | 4 210 |  |  |
| TOTAL | 35 800 | 38 670 | −7.4 |
| Persons engaged in: |  |  |  |
| Transport operation | 88 590 |  |  |
| Passenger traffic, commercial | 25 110 | 130 510 |  |
| Goods traffic, commercial | 5 880 |  |  |
| Materials | 38 560 | 46 890 |  |
| Equipment | 48 600 | 61 120 |  |
| TOTAL | 206 740 | 238 520 | −13.3 |
| Parcels service and road transport | 10 330 | 8 580 | +2.2 |
| SNCF total | 252 870 | 285 760 | −12 |

FRENCH RAILWAYS

|  | 1982 | 1972 | Percentage variation |
|---|---|---|---|
| Average number employed | 252 420 | 289 280 | −13 |
| Statutory hours of work | 1 736 | 1 925 | −9.8 |
| Absent for illness or injury, per 1000 | 27.7 | 29.7 | −6.73 |
| Total actual hours of work, millions | 424.5 | 540.4 | −21 |

## Productivity

|  | 1982 | 1972 | Percentage variation |
|---|---|---|---|
| Traffic-km per employee | 118.3 | 112.0 | +5.6 |
| Traffic-km | 278.7 | 207.3 | +34 |
| Tonne-km of gross weight hauled per hour of work | 608.0 | 471.7 | +29 |

# 6 Railways of the USA

It is difficult to establish which was the first *public* railway in the USA, as distinct from early wooden tracks serving industries. The Delaware & Hudson Canal Company obtained a railroad charter on 23 April 1823 for a line from Carbondale to the canal at Honesdale in the Lackawanna valley. The railroad, with a gauge of 1295 mm (4 ft 3 in), was opened on 9 October 1829. Although the company obtained a steam locomotive, *Stourbridge Lion*, from Foster, Rastrick & Company of Stourbridge, Worcestershire, England, it was too heavy for the wooden rails covered with iron strips, and the line was operated by horses until 1860.

The first railroad in the USA to offer a regular service as a public carrier was the Baltimore & Ohio Railroad, chartered on 28 February 1827. The first section, 21 km (13 miles) from Baltimore to Ellicott's Mills, Maryland, was opened for passengers and freight on 24 May 1830.

Growth and Decline of Railroad Route Length in USA

| Year | km | miles | Year | km | miles |
|------|------|------|------|------|------|
| 1830 | 37 | 23 | 1916 | 408 762 | 254 000 maximum |
| 1840 | 4 535 | 2 818 | 1920 | 406 935 | 252 865 |
| 1850 | 14 517 | 9 021 | 1930 | 401 711 | 249 619 |
| 1860 | 49 286 | 30 626 | 1940 | 376 869 | 234 182 |
| 1870 | 85 167 | 52 922 | 1950 | 361 015 | 224 331 |
| 1880 | 150 094 | 93 267 | 1960 | 350 104 | 217 551 |
| 1890 | 263 289 | 163 605 | 1970 | 336 345 | 209 001 |
| 1900 | 311 183 | 193 366 | 1975 | 320 453 | 199 126 |
| 1910 | 386 735 | 240 313 | 1980 | 294 625 | 183 077 |

A positive move to arrest the decline in quantity and quality of rail services was made by the Staggers Rail Act of 1980, passed 'to provide for the restoration, maintenance, and improvement of the physical qualities and financial stability of the rail system of the United States'.

The following table shows railway route length by States; taxes received by States from railroads; and number of railroad employees, 1980:

| State | km | miles | Tax received $000s | Employees |
|---|---|---|---|---|
| Alabama | 7 169 | 4 455 | 12 106 | 7 169 |
| Alaska | 885 | 550 | — | 716 |
| Arizona | 3 001 | 1 865 | 9 247 | 3 219 |
| Arkansas | 4 446 | 2 763 | 6 008 | 6 421 |
| California | 11 043 | 6 862 | 40 867 | 30 395 |
| Colorado | 5 573 | 3 463 | 7 887 | 6 902 |
| Connecticut | 1 025 | 637 | 304 | 3 441 |
| Delaware | 451 | 280 | 397 | 1 886 |
| District of Columbia | 88.5 | 55 | 704 | 2 769 |
| Florida | 5 924 | 3 681 | 2 079 | 11 019 |
| Georgia | 6 800 | 5 468 | 20 797 | 13 835 |
| Hawaii | — | — | 2 | — |
| Idaho | 3 883 | 2 413 | 5 795 | 3 214 |
| Illinois | 17 174 | 10 672 | 20 445 | 38 004 |
| Indiana | 9 572 | 5 948 | 8 984 | 13 461 |
| Iowa | 8 650 | 5 375 | 5 829 | 8 719 |
| Kansas | 11 693 | 7 266 | 16 365 | 15 143 |
| Kentucky | 5 657 | 3 515 | 9 355 | 14 209 |
| Louisiana | 5 428 | 3 373 | 2 106 | 9 051 |
| Maine | 2 393 | 1 487 | 1 585 | 2 111 |
| Maryland | 2 000 | 1 243 | 5 504 | 8 984 |
| Massachusetts | 2 345 | 1 457 | 2 669 | 4 418 |
| Michigan | 6 734 | 4 185 | 3 661 | 13 861 |
| Minnesota | 10 507 | 6 529 | 14 060 | 14 269 |
| Mississippi | 4 929 | 3 063 | 4 930 | 4 125 |
| Missouri | 9 831 | 6 109 | 11 818 | 15 247 |
| Montana | 6 139 | 3 815 | 8 801 | 6 422 |
| Nevada | 2 517 | 1 564 | 1 435 | 1 840 |
| New Hampshire | 964 | 599 | 356 | 586 |
| New Jersey | 2 586 | 1 607 | 3 483 | 7 494 |
| New Mexico | 3 339 | 2 075 | 2 512 | 3 224 |
| New York | 7 411 | 4 605 | 21 319 | 25 327 |

| State | km | miles | Tax received $000s | Employees |
|---|---|---|---|---|
| North Carolina | 5 756 | 3 577 | 12 634 | 7 076 |
| North Dakota | 7 992 | 4 966 | 5 504 | 3 223 |
| Ohio | 11 626 | 7 224 | 22 982 | 25 714 |
| Oklahoma | 6 324 | 3 930 | 4 588 | 3 208 |
| Oregon | 4 738 | 2 944 | 9 907 | 6 456 |
| Pennsylvania | 11 582 | 7 179 | 19 140 | 34 291 |
| Rhode Island | 235 | 146 | 1 580 | 601 |
| South Carolina | 4 403 | 2 736 | 7 733 | 3 742 |
| South Dakota | 2 830 | 1 759 | 230 | 917 |
| Tennessee | 5 047 | 3 136 | 13 543 | 10 087 |
| Texas | 21 425 | 13 313 | 12 893 | 29 311 |
| Utah | 2 665 | 1 656 | 7 362 | 4 600 |
| Vermont | 620 | 385 | 382 | 293 |
| Virginia | 5 637 | 3 503 | 21 215 | 13 933 |
| Washington | 7 045 | 4 378 | 9 145 | 8 941 |
| West Virginia | 5 737 | 3 565 | 11 174 | 8 260 |
| Wisconsin | 7 786 | 4 838 | 6 814 | 9 563 |
| Wyoming | 3 199 | 1 988 | 8 774 | 4 583 |
| TOTAL USA | 294 625 | 183 077 | 442 688 | 488 340 |

The famous 'hanging bridge' carrying the Denver & Rio Grande Western Railroad through the narrowest part of the Royal Gorge in Colorado, where it is over 300 m (1000 ft) deep, 3 August 1972. (John Marshall)

Denver & Rio Grande Western Railroad 914 mm (3 ft) gauge 2–8–0 No 318 (Baldwin 1896) and freight train at the Colorado Railroad Museum, Golden, 5 July 1970. (John Marshall)

Class K36 2–8–2 No 483 on an Antonito to Chama train at Cumbres station on the 914 mm (3 ft) gauge Cumbres & Toltec Scenic Railroad, Colorado, at 3053 m (10 015 ft) above sea level, 1 August 1972. (John Marshall)

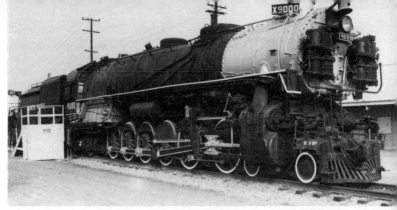

Union Pacific Railroad three-cylinder 4−12−2 No 9000, built at ALCO Brooks Works in 1926, first of a class of 88. Withdrawn in 1956. Now owned by the Southern California Chapter of the Railway & Locomotive Historical Society at Pomona Fairgrounds, Los Angeles. Photographed on 17 October 1983. (John Marshall)

The world's largest locomotive type, Union Pacific Railroad 4−8−8−4 'Big Boy', built by ALCO in 1941 and withdrawn in 1959. No 4014 is one of several preserved and is now owned by the same society at Pomona Fairgrounds, Los Angeles. (John Marshall)

The route length shown is that operated by Class I and Class II railroads only. Class I railroads are those with an annual operating revenue of $82 000 000 or more (1982). Figures for 1981 give Class I only, and so have not been used in this list.

From this table it will be seen that the state with the highest mileage is Texas, with 21 425 km (13 313 miles). The state which receives the greatest amount from railroad taxes is California, with $40 867 000. The state receiving the highest tax per mile of railroad (excluding Hawaii) is District of Columbia, $12 800 per mile. The state-owned Alaska Railroad pays no taxes. The state with the highest number of employees per mile is District of Columbia with 50.3 per mile; the lowest is North Dakota with 0.64 per mile.

The world's largest single-unit diesel-electric locomotive type, Union Pacific Railroad 'Centennial' class Do–Do No 6912, at Salt Lake City on 15 August 1977. (John Marshall)

## Principal Railway Systems of the USA

| Principal systems | km | miles |
|---|---:|---:|
| Alaska RR | 846 | 525 |
| Atchison, Topeka & Santa Fe RR | 19 571 | 12 160 |
| Boston & Maine Corporation | 2 279 | 1 416 |
| Burlington Northern | 44 052 | 27 374 |
| (Formed 2 March 1970 by the merging of: Chicago, Burlington & Quincy RR; Great Northern Railway; Northern Pacific Railway; Spokane, Portland & Seattle Railway. BN also operates the Colorado & Southern Railway and the Fort Worth & Denver Railway) | | |
| Chessie System Railroads, | 18 240 | 11 334 |
| comprising: Chesapeake & Ohio Railway | 7 820 | 4 680 |
| Baltimore & Ohio RR | 8 227 | 5 113 |
| Western Maryland Railway | 1 889 | 1 174 |
| Central Vermont Railway | 606 | 377 |
| Chicago, Milwaukee, St Paul & Pacific RR (Milwaukee Road) | 15 780 | 9 800 |
| Chicago & North Western RR | 12 302 | 7 646 |
| Consolidated Rail Corporation (Conrail) | 27 095 | 16 836 |
| Operating from 1 April 1976 and comprising: Central RR of New Jersey; Erie Lackawanna RR; Lehigh & Hudson River RR; Lehigh Valley RR; Penn Central (Pennsylvania + New York Central RRs); Reading RR | | |
| Denver & Rio Grande | 2 837 | 1 763 |
| Family Lines Rail System (Seaboard Coast Lines which merged in November 1980 with Chessie System to form CSX Corporation) | 26 185 | 16 270 |
| Florida East Coast Railway | 891 | 554 |
| Grand Trunk Western RR | 2 734 | 1 699 |
| Illinois Central Gulf RR | 12 812 | 7 963 |
| (Comprising former Illinois Central and Gulf, Mobile & Ohio RRs) | | |
| Kansas City Southern Lines | 1 419 | 882 |
| Long Island RR | 516 | 321 |

| Principal systems | km | miles |
|---|---|---|
| Maine Central RR | 1 316 | 818 |
| Missouri–Kansas–Texas RR | 3 499 | 2 174 |
| Missouri Pacific RR | 14 206 | 8 827 |
| Norfolk Southern RR | 28 742 | 17 860 |
| comprising: | | |
| Norfolk & Western RR | 12 555 | 7 803 |
| Southern RR | 16 185 | 10 057 |
| Pittsburgh & Lake Erie RR | 439 | 273 |
| Soo Line RR | 7 134 | 4 433 |
| Southern Pacific Transportation Co | 22 225 | 13 810 |
| St Louis Southwestern Railway | 3 939 | 2 448 |
| Union Pacific RR | 14 638 | 9 096 |
| Western Pacific RR | 2 390 | 1 486 |

As shown in the opposite table, although the number of freight cars declined by 39 per cent from 1929 to 1982, the total carrying capacity increased by 7.3 per cent because of larger cars of improved design. New cars put into service in 1982 had an average capacity of 91 tons. At the end of 1981 the aggregate capacity of the fleet was about 13 447 422 tons, about 11.5 per cent higher than in 1971. The decline in the number of freight car loads is a result of the increased car capacity. Revenue ton-miles per loaded car increased about five-fold from 1929 to 1982; in the last decade the average rose by 44 per cent, again as a result of larger, specialised freight cars and longer average hauls. Revenue ton miles reached a peak of 918 621 million in 1980.

The number of cars in the average freight train is calculated by dividing freight car-miles by freight train-miles. The average freight train load represents net ton-miles per freight train-mile. Ton-miles are the product of load in tons and distance transported in miles. In 1981–2, ton-miles per loaded car increased by 2.3 per cent. Freight train miles over the 177 012 miles of route used in freight service averaged 6.3 train miles per day per mile of route.

## US Freight Traffic

| | 1929 | 1939 | 1947 | 1955 | 1967 | 1975 | 1982 |
|---|---|---|---|---|---|---|---|
| 1 Freight cars | 2 610 622 | 1 961 705 | 2 025 008 | 1 996 443 | 1 822 381 | 1 723 605 | 1 587 537 |
| 2 Cars per average freight train | 47.6 | 48.1 | 52.2 | 65.5 | 70.5 | 68.6 | 69.1 |
| 3 Average freight car capacity, tons | 46.3 | 49.7 | 51.5 | 53.7 | 63.4 | 72.9 | 81.7 |
| 4 Average freight car load, tons | 35.4 | 36.8 | 41.0 | 42.4 | 51.1 | 60.8 | 68.3 |
| 5 Average freight train load, tons | 804 | 806 | 1 131 | 1 359 | 1 740 | 1 938 | 2 345 |
| 6 Freight car loadings | 52 827 925 | 33 911 498 | 44 502 188 | 37 636 031 | 28 083 751 | 23 217 158 | 18 550 199 |
| 7 Revenue ton-miles per loaded car | 8468 | 9833 | 14 712 | 16 570 | 25 620 | 32 487 | 43 005 |
| 8 Revenue ton-miles, millions (Class I railroads only) | 447 322 | 333 438 | 654 728 | 623 615 | 719 498 | 754 252 | 797 759 |
| 9 Freight train miles, 1000s | 613 444 | 451 991 | 616 071 | 476 444 | 420 365 | 402 557 | 203 176 |
| 10 Average haul per ton, miles | 317.17 | 351.21 | 407.82 | 429.75 | 485.21 | 515.89 | c 604.00 |

**Freight Commodities**

|  | Tons 000s | % of total | Car loadings 000s 1982 | 1981 |
|---|---|---|---|---|
| Coal | 523 823 | 41.3 | 5 660 | 5 762 |
| Farm products | 133 521 | 10.5 | 1 484 | 1 576 |
| Metallic ores | 62 620 | 4.9 | 824 | 1 607 |
| Non-metallic minerals | 84 724 | 6.7 | 503 | 675 |
| Chemicals and allied products | 91 182 | 7.2 | 1 116 | 1 349 |
| Food and kindred products | 76 959 | 6.0 | 682 | 784 |
| Lumber and wood products (excluding furniture) | 65 863 | 5.2 | 305 | 397 |
| Primary metal products | 32 004 | 2.5 | 458 | 786 |
| Stone, clay and glass products | 38 170 | 3.0 | 509 | 690 |
| Pulp, paper and allied products | 36 421 | 2.9 | 828 | 991 |
| Petroleum and coal products (including coke) | 31 648 | 2.5 | 476 | 599 |
| Waste and scrap material | 22 733 | 1.8 | 405 | 606 |

**Types of Freight Equipment**

| | |
|---|---|
| Box cars, plain | 190 620 |
| equipped | 162 349 |
| Covered hoppers | 306 222 |
| Flat cars | 144 508 |
| Refrigerator cars | 68 043 |
| Gondola cars | 176 931 |
| Hopper cars | 325 642 |
| Tank cars | 185 838 |
| Other freight cars | 27 384 |
| TOTAL[1] 1982 | 1 587 537 |

[1] This total does not include about 13 000 cabooses.

Piggyback traffic (road trailers on rail flat cars) rose from 249 065 revenue cars in 1957 to a peak of 1 920 377 in 1982. In 1981 it was 1 723 410, 3.8 per cent above 1980 but 7.2 per cent below the 1979 record. The number of trailers and trailer-size containers loaded totalled 3 396 973, a gain of 7.8 per cent over 1981.

## Intercity Freight and Passenger Traffic

Millions of revenue freight ton-miles and percentage of total

|  | Ton-miles | | Percentage | |
|  | 1929 | 1982 | 1929 | 1982 |
|---|---|---|---|---|
| Railroads (all classes) | 454 800 | 812 000 | 74.9 | 36.3 |
| Trucks | 19 689 | 506 000 | 3.3 | 22.7 |
| Great Lakes | 97 322 | 88 000 | 16.0 | 3.9 |
| Rivers and canals | 8 661 | 287 000 | 1.4 | 12.9 |
| Oil pipe lines | 26 900 | 537 000 | 4.4 | 24.0 |
| Air | 3 | 5 000 | — | 0.2 |
| TOTAL | 607 375 | 1 235 000 | | |

Millions of revenue passenger-miles and percentage of total (except private)

|  | Passenger-miles | | Percentage | |
|  | 1929 | 1982 | 1929 | 1982 |
|---|---|---|---|---|
| Railroads | 33 965 | 10 900 | 77.1 | 4.3 |
| Buses | 6 800 | 28 000 | 15.4 | 10.9 |
| Air | — | 213 000 | — | 83.2 |
| Inland waterways | 3 300 | 4 000 | 7.5 | 1.6 |
| TOTAL (except private) | 44 065 | 255 900 | | |
| Private cars | 175 000 | 1 371 000 | | |
| Private aircraft | — | 14 500 | | |
| TOTAL (including private) | 219 065 | 1 641 700 | | |
| Average journey per passenger (miles) | 39.63 | 36.63 (1980) | | |

## Numbers of Passenger Train Cars

| Dec 31 | US total | Pullman Co (included in total) |
|--------|----------|-------------------------------|
| 1929 | 61 728 | 9 469 |
| 1939 | 45 479 | 7 052 |
| 1947 | 44 841 | 6 071 |
| 1955 | 36 871 | 4 776 |
| 1967 | 18 610 | 1 021 |
| 1968 | 15 384 | 765 |
| 1969 | 12 426 | — |
| | | Amtrak |
| 1971 | 8 713 | 1 165 |
| 1975 | 6 471 | 1 913 |
| 1980 | 4 347 | 2 128 |
| 1982 | 3 736 | 1 929 |

The National Railroad Passenger Corporation, known as 'Amtrak', was formed under the Rail Passenger Service Act of 31 October 1970. It took over the passenger services of 22 of the leading railroads of the USA. Operations began on 1 May 1971. The principal companies remaining outside were the Southern, Denver & Rio Grande Western, and the Rock Island & Pacific. Amtrak now operates about 200 trains daily over 37 970 km (23 594 miles) of route connecting 440 cities in the USA and into Canada. It owns 396 locomotives and 1929 passenger cars. In 1982 it carried 18 177 534 revenue passengers a total of 6 425 793 000 km (3 992 912 000 miles). Average passenger journey was 353.5 km (219.66 miles). Passenger train-km totalled 46 401 729 (28 833 486 train-miles); car-km totalled 349 837 680 (217 385 000 car-miles).

## Locomotives in Service

|                | 1929   | 1939   | 1947   | 1955   | 1967   | 1975   | 1982   |
| -------------- | ------ | ------ | ------ | ------ | ------ | ------ | ------ |
| Steam          | 56 936 | 41 117 | 35 108 | 5 982  | 21     | 12     | 2      |
| Diesel-electric | 22    | 510    | 5 772  | 24 786 | 27 309 | 27 985 | 27 000 |
| Electric       | 601    | 843    | 821    | 627    | 321    | 213    | 71     |
| TOTAL          | 57 559 | 42 470 | 41 701 | 31 395 | 27 651 | 28 210 | 27 073 |

## Age of Locomotives at 31 December 1982

|             | Number | Percentage |
| ----------- | ------ | ---------- |
| Before 1960 | 7 264  | 27.1       |
| 1960–64     | 2 238  | 8.3        |
| 1965–69     | 4 889  | 18.2       |
| 1970–74     | 5 282  | 19.7       |
| 1975–79     | 5 063  | 18.9       |
| 1980–82     | 2 100  | 7.8        |

Transcontinental train on the Canadian National route in Jasper National Park, Alberta. (Canadian National Railways)

# 7 Canadian Railways

Unlike Europe, where railways had to be fitted into communities established for many centuries, in Canada the story of railway development is almost synonymous with that of the development of the country. The first railway in Canada about which there is any positive information was a double-track balanced incline 152 m (500 ft) long, built by the Royal Engineers in 1823 to carry stone from a wharf on the St Lawrence to the top of the escarpment at Quebec during construction of the Citadel. It was worked by a horse gin, but later references to boiler repairs suggest that the gin may have been replaced by a steam engine, and that it lasted into the 1830s.

Coal-carrying railways were built in Nova Scotia at Pictou in 1827 and North Sydney in 1828. Both used horses. They were standard, 1435 mm (4 ft 8½ in), gauge and were probably the first in North America to use iron rails, which were cast in 1524 mm (5 ft) lengths. Canada's first steam railway was a standard-gauge line 26.5 km (16¼ miles) long operated by 'The Company of Proprietors of the Champlain & Saint Lawrence Rail Road', chartered in 1832. It was opened from Laprairie on the St Lawrence to St John on the Richelieu on 21 July 1836.

These railways were followed by the standard-gauge Albion Colliery Tramway and the Erie & Ontario in 1839, and the Montreal & Lachine Railroad built to a gauge of 1448 mm (4 ft 9 in).

In 1845 the Province of Canada appointed a Royal Commission to study the railway gauge question but, until the financing of a 'main line' became a major issue, the Commission was slow in consulting various authorities. In the meantime the St Lawrence & Atlantic Rail Road which, with the Atlantic & St Lawrence Rail Road in USA, linked Montreal with Portland, Maine, to provide an ice-free port for Montreal in winter, was built to a gauge of 1676 mm (5 ft 6 in) and opened in 1847–52.

Despite a majority of professional opinion against the broad gauge, the Commission recommended the gauge of 1676 mm in deference to economic and political developments. On 31 July 1851 the Province of Canada legislated to make this 'Provincial Gauge' a pre-condition of financial assistance, so strengthening the Guarantee Act of 1849.

The Grand Trunk Railway was incorporated in 1852 by an Act which amalgamated the Quebec & Richmond; St Lawrence & Atlantic; Old Grand Trunk; Grand Junction; Toronto, Guelph & Sarnia; and Main Trunk, with a total length of 2216 km (1377 miles).

The Great Western Railway of Canada was empowered by various Acts between 1834 and 1858 to build a line from Niagara Falls to Windsor, Ontario, opposite Detroit, via Hamilton and London, 369 km (229 miles). The main line was begun at London in 1847 and the company was forced to adopt the broad gauge before opening from Niagara Falls to London in 1853 and to Windsor in 1855, but it installed a third rail on the main line in 1867 to provide standard gauge. The total length was 555 km (345 miles) comprising main line 369 km (229 miles); Hamilton–Toronto 61 km (38 miles); Galt branch 19 km (12 miles); Sarnia branch 82 km (51 miles).

The growth of the standard and broad gauges in the Province of Canada from 1836 to 1860 is shown in the table below. By 1860 92 per cent of the 3476 km (2160 miles) of public railway in Canada, New Brunswick and Nova Scotia was broad gauge.

| Year | 1 435 mm km | 1 676 mm km | Total km | miles |
|------|------|------|------|------|
| 1836 | 23 | | 23 | 14 |
| 1847 | 35 | 48 | 83 | 52 |
| 1850 | 55 | 48 | 103 | 64 |
| 1851 | 90 | 48 | 138 | 86 |
| 1852 | 151 | 154 | 305 | 190 |
| 1853 | 151 | 496 | 647 | 402 |
| 1854 | 238 | 940 | 1 178 | 632 |
| 1855 | 238 | 1 320 | 1 558 | 968 |
| 1856 | 238 | 2 023 | 2 261 | 1 405 |
| 1857 | 238 | 2 116 | 2 354 | 1 463 |
| 1858 | 238 | 2 343 | 2 581 | 1 604 |
| 1859 | 283 | 2 699 | 2 982 | 1 853 |
| 1860 | 283 | 2 745 | 3 028 | 1 882 |

By the time of the Confederation of Nova Scotia, New Brunswick, Quebec and Ontario to form the nucleus of the Dominion of Canada on 1 July 1867 there were 15 railways totalling 4015 km (2495 miles), employing 9391 persons. There were 485 locomotives, 310 first class and 374 second class passenger cars which carried a total of 2 920 000 passengers in the year, and 4214 freight cars which carried 2 260 000 tons.

The Intercolonial Railway was incorporated on 12 April 1867. A condition of the Confederation was the building of a railway from Halifax, Nova Scotia, through New Brunswick to the Saint Lawrence at or near Quebec, to be started within six months. For economic and military reasons the railway followed a route via Campbellton on the Bay of Chaleur and across to the St Lawrence which it followed up to Rivière du Loup. Much of the system, throughout Nova Scotia and into New Brunswick, was built to the broad gauge. Halifax to Truro opened in 1858, Truro to Amherst in 1872. The main line from near Newcastle, New Brunswick, to Trois Pistoles on the St Lawrence, about 467 km (290 miles), was built to standard gauge. Amherst to Rivière du Loup on the St Lawrence was opened on 1 July 1876. By then the broad-gauge line from Levis, opposite Quebec, to Rivière du Loup had been built by the Grand Trunk; it was acquired by the Intercolonial in 1879.

The Dominion Government repealed the Provincial Gauge in 1870, by which time most Canadian and USA Railways had adopted standard gauge. Conversion of the Grand Trunk Railway took until 1874. The Intercolonial between Halifax and Truro (and St John) was converted to standard gauge by 1875 and the remainder of the route soon afterwards; so, by 1876 a standard-gauge line connected Halifax and Levis.

Prince Edward Island entered the Confederation in 1873 while its railway system was under construction. The 338 km (210 miles) of route were taken over by the Federal Government and opened for traffic in April 1875. Railways on Prince Edward Island grew to a total of 448 km (297 miles), all standard gauge.

In 1882 the Grand Trunk and Great Western Railways were amalgamated with a total of 1455 km (904 miles) of route, together with another 761 km (473 miles) of line in Western Ontario.

The Grand Trunk Western Railroad was formed in 1893 by amalgamation of the Grand Trunk properties in the State of Michigan to provide a through route to Chicago.

Congestion on the Canadian Pacific Railway (to be mentioned later) between Winnipeg and Fort William on Lake Superior, and a desire by the GTR for a share in the long-haul traffic to the Pacific, led to proposals for a second transcontinental route. After unsuccessful attempts to extend westwards through the USA, the GTR agreed in 1900 that the Government should build the Eastern Division of the National Transcontinental Railway between Moncton and Winnipeg and that the newly-created Grand Trunk Pacific Railway, as a subsidiary of the GTR, should build from there to the

Pacific coast at Prince Rupert, 885 km (550 miles) north of Vancouver. With government aid the GTP was built to the same high standards as the GTR had been.

Both the National Transcontinental Eastern Division and the Grand Trunk Pacific were begun in 1905. The National Transcontinental was opened in stages from June to November 1915. It included the great Quebec Bridge over the St Lawrence, not opened until 1917. The GTP was completed at a point 671 km (417 miles) east of Prince Rupert on 7 April 1914 and full services began in September.

From Winnipeg the GTP passed through Edmonton and through the Yellowhead Pass by which it made the lowest crossing of the Rockies, with the easiest grades, of any North American transcontinental railway.

With the Canadian Pacific, Canada now had two transcontinental railways, with ample capacity for its transport requirements. The 'necessity' for a third was the invention of two men, William Mackenzie (1849–1923) and Donald Mann (1853–1934), who projected the Canadian Northern Railway. Its history began in 1896 with the acquisition by Mackenzie and Mann of the Lake Manitoba Railway & Canal Company. Sections of new construction and further acquisitions of separately incorporated railways brought the total route in 1903 to 554 km (344 miles) in the east, and to 2192 km (1362 miles) in the west. By 1905 the western lines had reached Edmonton and Prince Albert, and in the east Hawkesbury was linked to Ottawa. Surveys through the Yellowhead Pass began in 1908 and on 4 October 1915 the Canadian Northern was opened to Vancouver, through the Fraser River Canyon which it shared with the Canadian Pacific. The Canadian Northern had now grown to 15 067 km (9362 miles) and extended from Quebec to Vancouver, with additional lines in Nova Scotia and in the USA (the Duluth, Winnipeg & Pacific).

In 1917, to aid the war effort, over 161 km (100 miles) each of the Grand Trunk Pacific and Canadian Northern tracks were removed between Lobstick Junction, Alberta, through the Yellowhead Pass, to Red Pass Junction where the Prince Rupert and Vancouver lines diverged, to make a joint line of the two competing sections.

One of the last and largest works on the Canadian Northern was the Mount Royal Tunnel, 5073 m (3 miles 268 yd), which carried the line directly into Montreal. It was opened on 21 October 1918. Soon after the transcontinental line was opened the Canadian Northern was in financial difficulties and, following careful consideration by the Government, **Canadian National Railways** was formed to acquire the Canadian Northern Railway. In 1919 the Grand Trunk Pacific was allowed to go into receivership. On 21 May 1920 the Government took formal possession of the Grand Trunk Railway and in September 1920 met the debenture obligations as *de facto* proprietor of the Grand Trunk Pacific. The Grand Trunk Acquisition Act was passed on 5 November 1920. In 1923, under an Order in Council, the control of all government railways including the Grand Trunk and the Intercolonial Railways passed to the Canadian National Railways under a president and board of directors appointed by the Government.

In 1949 the Newfoundland Railway was absorbed, adding 1135 km (750 miles) of 1067 mm (3 ft 6 in) gauge route. Of this, 880 km (547 miles) were on the main 'Overland Route' from St John's to Port aux Basques.

In 1923 the Canadian National Railways had 33 109 km (20 573 miles) of route, one of the world's largest railway systems. Today the CN serves all ten provinces, and a branch reaches Churchill on Hudson Bay in Manitoba. North of Edmonton the Northern Alberta Railway, joint CPR and CN, operates 1485 km (923 miles) of route and from Roma Junction near Peace River on this system CN operates the Great Slave Lake Railway, 607 km (377 miles), opened in 1964 to the Great Slave Lake in North West Territories. The CN offers one of the world's longest railway journeys: Halifax, Nova Scotia, to Montreal 1352 km (840 miles), and Montreal to Prince Rupert 4998 km (3105 miles), total 6350 km (3946 miles).

CN also operates a highway transport service, coastal steamers, a chain of large hotels, and a telecommunications service. Air Canada, an autonomous subsidiary of CN, operates Canadian and International air services.

In 1982 CN freight traffic totalled 125 257 million ton-km. Rolling stock consisted of 2162 diesel-electric locomotives, 14 electric locomotives (operating on 63 km (39 miles) of electrified route at 2.7 kV) and 92 077 freight cars. The now familiar CN monogram was adopted in 1960.

The oldest charter of a constituent of the **Canadian Pacific Railway** was that incorporating the St Andrews & Quebec Railroad Company in March 1836 for a railway from St Andrews, New Brunswick, to Lower Canada. The oldest operating constituent of the CPR was La Compagnie du Chemin à Rails du Saint Laurent et du Village d'Industrie, 19 km (12 miles) long from Village d'Industrie (now Joliette, Quebec) to Lanoraie on the St Lawrence about 56 km (35 miles) north-east of Montreal. Regular services began on 6 May 1850. It came into the possession of what is now CP Rail with the purchase of the Eastern Division of the Quebec, Montreal, Ottawa & Occidental Railway in September 1885, and part of it is still in use.

The Canadian Pacific transcontinental line, the first railway across Canada, was completed at a place named Craigellachie in Eagle Pass, British Columbia, when the Eastern and Western sections were joined on 7 November 1885. Its completion within ten years was a condition of British

Columbia entering the Confederation, on 20 July 1871. The first sod was cut on 1 June 1875 at Fort William on the left bank of the Kaministiquia River. The main contract was signed on 21 October 1880 by which year 1126 km (700 miles) were under construction. The Canadian Pacific Railway Company was incorporated on 15 February 1881; construction began on 2 May 1881, and throughout 1882 4 km (2.5 miles) of track were laid every day. The Prairie section was finished as far as Calgary on 18 August 1883 and the Great Lakes section on 16 May 1885, thanks to the devotion and energy of William Cornelius Van Horne (qv). The section through the rock and muskeg north of Lake Superior was almost as difficult as the construction through the British Columbia mountains.

Transcontinental services began with the departure of the first train from Montreal on 28 June 1886. It arrived at Port Moody on 4 July. The 19.3 km (12 miles) extension to Vancouver was opened on 23 May 1887. From Montreal to Vancouver, 4633 km (2879 miles), takes three days.

Today, of the six departments of Canadian Pacific Ltd, **CP Rail** controls the former CPR lines; **CP Transport** operates Canada's largest trucking service; **CP Telecommunications** provides a transmission service to business and industry throughout Canada; **CP Hotels** has hotels in Canada, Mexico and Germany; **CP Ships** maintains a fast containerised service between Canada and Europe; **CP Air** operates 84 800 km (52 700 miles) of domestic and overseas routes.

In 1982 CP Rail hauled 77 million tons of freight, 86 300 million ton-km. Rolling stock consisted of 1300 diesel locomotives, 60 000 freight cars and 3900 miscellaneous work vehicles.

In the west the British Columbia Railway operates 2063 km (1281 miles) of route from North Vancouver to Fort Nelson. The first section was opened in 1921 and it was completed to Fort Nelson in September 1971. It owns 82 diesel locomotives, 4441 freight cars and 6 diesel-hydraulic railcars. The Ontario Northland Railway, owned by the Government of Ontario, operates a line from the CN and CP lines at North Bay, north of Toronto, 708 km (440 miles) to Moosonee on James Bay with other lines making a total of 954 km (593 miles). Its rolling stock comprises 38 diesel locomotives, 45 passenger cars, 967 freight cars and 203 miscellaneous vehicles. In the north east the Quebec North Shore & Labrador Railway connects iron ore mines at Shefferville with the north shore of the St Lawrence at Sept-Iles by a standard-gauge line 574 km (357 miles) long, opened in 1954, with 81 diesel locomotives, 554 freight cars and 446 miscellaneous cars. Total route lengths of the various Canadian systems are shown on p 42).

CN made the largest contribution to Canada's total railway revenue in 1977, of 53.9 per cent. CP Rail came next with 36 per cent; the Quebec North

Shore & Labrador 2.1 per cent; British Columbia Railway 2.3 per cent; Ontario Northland 1.2 per cent.

**VIA Rail Canada** was incorporated on 12 January 1977 for the purpose of revitalising rail passenger services, to manage and to market them on an efficient commercial basis, so reducing the financial burden on the government. The first joint CP/CN timetable was issued, under the VIA symbol, in October 1976. VIA purchased all CN and CP Rail's passenger equipment in 1978. From 1 April 1979 VIA assumed full financial responsibility for the passenger services formerly operated by CN and CP Rail. In 1981 8 million passenger journeys were made; a total of 3115 million passenger-km. VIA rolling stock at the end of 1982 comprised: 164 diesel locomotives; 85 diesel railcars; 14 turbo cars; 788 coaches.

## Railway Development in Canada

| Year | km | miles | Year | km | miles |
|------|------|------|------|------|------|
| 1840 | 26 | 16 | 1940 | 68 502 | 42 565 |
| 1850 | 106 | 66 | 1950[1] | 69 168 | 42 979 |
| 1860 | 3 323 | 2 065 | 1960 | 70 858 | 44 029 |
| 1870 | 4 212 | 2 617 | 1970 | 70 784 | 43 983 |
| 1880 | 11 577 | 7 194 | 1971 | 71 057 | 44 153 |
| 1890 | 21 164 | 13 151 | 1972 | 70 851 | 44 025 |
| 1900 | 28 415 | 17 657 | 1973 | 71 185 | 44 232 |
| 1910 | 39 801 | 24 731 | 1974 | 71 239 | 44 266 |
| 1920 | 62 451 | 38 805 | 1975 | 70 716 | 43 941 |
| 1930 | 67 668 | 42 047 | 1980 | 69 340 | 43 086 |

[1] Newfoundland included from 1950.

## Railway Route Lengths of Lines in Canadian Provinces and of Canadian Lines in USA, 1977

|  | km | miles |
|------|------|------|
| Newfoundland | 1 473 | 915 |
| Prince Edward Island | 408 | 254 |
| Nova Scotia | 1 968 | 1 223 |
| New Brunswick | 2 641 | 1 641 |
| Quebec | 8 570 | 5 325 |

| | km | miles |
|---|---|---|
| Ontario | 15 732 | 9 775 |
| Manitoba | 7 363 | 4 575 |
| Saskatchewan | 13 518 | 8 400 |
| Alberta | 9 670 | 6 009 |
| British Columbia | 7 686 | 4 776 |
| Yukon Territory | 93 | 58 |
| Northwest Territories | 208 | 129 |
| United States | 637 | 396 |
| TOTAL route length | 69 967 | 43 475 |
| TOTAL trackage | 94 987 | 59 022 |

**Canadian Rolling Stock, all Railways, in Service at 31 December 1977**

| *Locomotives:* | | Self-propelled cars | 116 |
|---|---|---|---|
| Steam | — | Coaches | 733 |
| Diesel-electric | 4 021 | Combination | 31 |
| Electric | 14 | Dining cars | 75 |
| | | Parlour cars | 116 |
| TOTAL | 4 035 | Sleeping cars | 291 |
| *Passenger cars:* | | Baggage, postal and | |
| Turbo-train power units | 6 | express cars | 359 |
| coaches | 15 | Other | 5 |
| parlour cars | 6 | TOTAL | 1 753 |

Several railway preservation societies and privately owned preserved lines operate steam locomotives and old rolling stock.

| *Freight cars:* | | | |
|---|---|---|---|
| Automobile | 3 411 | Refrigerator | 4 685 |
| Ballast | 2 652 | Stock | 1 924 |
| Box | 83 478 | Tank | 324 |
| Flat | 25 081 | Other | 3 289 |
| Gondola | 20 291 | TOTAL | 187 183 |
| Hopper | 33 387 | | |
| Ore | 8 661 | | |

*Privately owned cars:*

| | |
|---|---|
| Tank | 14 107 |
| Other | 13 623 |
| TOTAL | 27 730 |

## Commodities Hauled as Revenue Freight by Canadian Railways in 1977 (thousands of tonnes)

*Live animals:*

| | |
|---|---|
| Cattle | 87 |
| Other live animals | 6 |
| TOTAL | 93 |

*Food, feed, beverages, etc:*

| | |
|---|---|
| Meat, fresh or frozen | 212 |
| Other animal products | 171 |
| Barley | 4 163 |
| Wheat | 17 924 |
| Other grains | 2 163 |
| Milled cereals and cereal products | 1 988 |
| Fruits and fruit preparations | 639 |
| Vegetables and vegetable preparations | 1 175 |
| Sugar | 379 |
| Other food and food preparations | 775 |
| Animal feed | 2 532 |
| Beverages | 349 |
| Tobacco and tobacco products | 44 |
| TOTAL | 32 514 |

*Crude materials:*

| | |
|---|---|
| Crude animal and vegetable materials | 2 003 |
| Pulpwood (logs and chips) | 10 390 |
| Other crude wood materials | 2 563 |
| Textile fibres | 97 |
| Iron ore | 57 288 |
| Nickel, copper ore | 5 214 |
| Bauxite ore and alumina | 2 585 |
| Other metallic ores | 6 396 |
| Scrap metal, slags and drosses | 1 644 |
| Coal | 19 277 |
| Crude oil and bituminous substances | 302 |
| Gypsum | 4 359 |
| Limestone | 3 507 |
| Other crude non-metallic minerals | 12 754 |
| Waste materials | 730 |
| TOTAL | 129 109 |

*Wood products, chemicals, etc:*

| | |
|---|---|
| Lumber | 8 146 |
| Other wood fabricated materials | 2 008 |
| Wood pulp and other pulp | 5 316 |
| Newsprint | 4 075 |
| Other paper and paper board | 3 074 |
| Chemicals | 6 376 |
| Potash | 8 719 |
| Other fertilisers | 2 401 |
| Petroleum and coal products | 12 432 |
| Metals and primary metal products | 5 403 |

| | | | | |
|---|---|---|---|---|
| Cement | 1 931 | *Special traffic:* | | |
| Other fabricated materials | 4 382 | Piggyback (trailers and | | |
| | | containers) | | 7 156 |
| TOTAL | 64 263 | Freight forwarder | | 1 680 |
| | | Other special traffic | | 2 147 |
| *End products:* | | | | |
| Road motor vehicles and | | TOTAL | | 10 983 |
| parts | 5 843 | Non carload shipments | | 1 037 |
| Other end products | 3 403 | | | |
| | | TOTAL commodities | | 247 247 |
| TOTAL | 9 246 | | | |

The above table does not include operations over Canadian railways in the USA except for the CPR line through Maine; but it does include sections of USA railways operating in Canada.

# 8 Australian Railways

Railway development in Australia was on a piecemeal basis, each colony forming its own policy without regard to future unification. Apart from early tramways, Australia's first steam-operated railway was a 1600 mm (5 ft 3 in) gauge line from Melbourne to Sandridge in Victoria, opened on 12 September 1854. The first passenger railway was the 11 km (7 mile) Port Elliot & Goolwa Railway in South Australia, on 18 May 1854, also 1600 mm.

In New South Wales the 'standard' or 1435 mm (4 ft 8½ in) gauge was adopted for the first railway from Sydney to Panamatta Junction, now Granville, opened on 26 September 1855, by which date it had been taken over by the New South Wales Government.

South Australia adopted the 1600 mm gauge for its first railway from Adelaide to Port Adelaide opened on 21 April 1856. It was built and worked by the South Australian Government. Largely for cheapness of construction, Queensland adopted a gauge of 1067 mm (3 ft 6 in) for the first railway, opened in July 1865 between Ipswich and Grandchester, 35 km (20¼ miles). Tasmania's first railway, completed in 1871 from Launceston to Deloraine, was built to 1600 mm gauge. In 1872 it was taken over by the government as was the later Launceston–Hobart line opened in 1876. In 1888 the lines were converted to 1067 mm gauge which had been adopted as the Tasmanian gauge. Western Australia also adopted the 1067 mm gauge. Its first railway was a private line built in 1871 from near Busselton into the nearby forest for the transport of timber.

In 1889 another isolated 1067 mm line came into use from Darwin, in Northern Territory, southwards for 233 km (145 miles) to Pine Creek. It was extended 85 km (53 miles) to Emungalan in 1917, 105 km (65 miles) to Mataranka in 1928 and 82 km (51 miles) to Larrimah just north of Birdum in 1929, a total of 503 km (312 miles), leaving a gap of 1000 km (622 miles) to Alice Springs, terminus of the Central Australian Railway. This 1067 mm gauge line from Marree to Alice Springs was closed on 1 January 1981 following the opening, on 9 October 1980, of a new standard-gauge line to Alice Springs from Tarcola on the Trans-Australian Railway.

Services between Darwin and Larrimah on the North Australian Railway were withdrawn on 30 June 1976 and the line was officially closed on 11 February 1981. In 1981 the Commonwealth Government announced its intention to build a standard-gauge railway 1500 km (932 miles) long from Alice Springs to Darwin, expected to be completed in 1988.

By the time of the constitution of the Australian Commonwealth, on 9 July 1900, Australia had 20 126 km (12 506 miles) of railway of three gauges.

Route-kilometres of government-owned railways of three gauges in States and Territories on 30 June 1979 are listed in the following table. Some state systems operate over the border into neighbouring states. The table shows simply route lengths in each state.

| State | 1 600 mm | 1 435 mm | 1 067 mm | Total km |
|-------|----------|----------|----------|----------|
| New South Wales | 328[1] | 9 820[2] | — | 10 148 |
| Victoria | 5 531 | 325[3] | — | 5 856 |
| Queensland | — | 111 | 9 678 | 9 789 |
| South Australia | 2 537[4] | 1 871 | 1 536 | 5 944 |
| Western Australia | — | 2 108 | 4 393[5] | 6 501 |
| Tasmania | — | — | 864 | 864 |
| Northern Territory | — | — | 278 | 278 |
| Australian Capital Territory | — | 8 | — | 8 |
| Australian total | 8 396 | 14 243 | 16 749 | 39 388 |

[1] Part of Victorian Railways system.
[2] Includes 47 km of 1435 mm gauge line from Broken Hill to Cockburn operated by Australian National Railways.
[3] Includes 12 km of 1435/1600 mm dual-gauge line which operates in the Melbourne metropolitan area.
[4] Includes 142 km of the Adelaide metropolitan railway system operated by South Australian State Transport Authority.
[5] Excludes 148 km of 1067/1435 mm dual-gauge line which is included in the 1435 mm gauge length.

From this table it will be clear that conversion of the Australian government railways to standard gauge, which forms only 36.16 per cent of the total, is no simple matter. There have been several government reports, since the first in 1857, recommending unification of the Australian railways on the standard gauge.

The standard-gauge Trans-Australian Railway was opened on 22 October 1917, connecting two 1067 mm gauge systems at Kalgoorlie, Western

Australia, and Port Augusta, South Australia. The first positive step towards unification was made on 27 September 1930 when the extension of the New South Wales Government Railways coast line was opened from Kyogle into South Brisbane, Queensland.

During World War II the need for unification became more urgent, and on 24 March 1945 a report was published by Sir Harold Clapp, former Commissioner of the Victorian Railways and wartime Director General of the Australian Commonwealth Transport Board. He outlined a seven-year plan for conversion to standard gauge of the 1600 mm South Australian and Victorian systems and the 1067 mm gauge of South Australia together with construction of a new standard-gauge line from Kalgoorlie to Fremantle via Perth in Western Australia. The high estimated cost was probably the main reason for failure to implement the recommendations.

In 1956 a Federal parliamentary committee, formed to investigate a scheme to convert only the main routes, recommended that standard-gauge lines be built from Albury to Melbourne, Broken Hill to Adelaide via Port Pirie, and Kalgoorlie to Fremantle via Perth.

In 1957 the Australian, New South Wales and Victorian governments agreed on the construction of a standard-gauge line parallel to the existing 1600 mm gauge line between Albury and Melbourne. Under the agreement the Commonwealth was to meet 70 per cent and each state 15 per cent of the cost. The state's portion was advanced by the Commonwealth, to be repaid with interest over 50 years. The new line cost \$31 946 000 and was opened in 1962. With the conversion of the Kalgoorlie–Perth section and of the section from Port Pirie to Broken Hill from 1067 mm to standard gauge, completed on 29 November 1969, a through route entirely on standard gauge was opened up from Perth to Sydney, 3960 km (2461 miles). The section from Perth to Northern is dual gauged. The 'Indian Pacific Express' was inaugurated on 1 March 1970 by the opening of the new standard-gauge route from Sydney to Perth. The 'Indian Pacific' runs four times a week each way, taking $2\frac{3}{4}$ days.

Distances by rail between Sydney and the other capital cities are: Canberra 327 km (203 miles); Brisbane via North Coast line 987 km (613 miles); Brisbane via Wallangarra 1151 km (715 miles); Melbourne 959 km (596 miles); Adelaide via Melbourne 1736 km (1079 miles); Perth via Broken Hill 3961 km (2461 miles); Perth via Melbourne 4367 km (2714 miles).

There are six government-owned railway systems operated by the State Railway Authority of New South Wales (SRA); Queensland Government Railways (QR); Victorian Railways (VR); Western Australian Government Railways (WAGR); State Transport Authority of South Australia (STA); and Australian National Railways (ANR).

The approximate number of persons employed on Australian Railways in 1978–9 was as follows:

| | |
|---|---|
| New South Wales | 42 765 |
| Victoria | 23 277 |
| Queensland | 24 667 |
| South Australia | 3 790[1] |
| Western Australia | 9 713 |
| Australian National | 11 049 |
| Australian total | 115 140 |

[1] Includes details for combined rail, bus and tram operations. Separate details for rail are not available. Also includes staff on loan from and paid by the Australian National Railways Commission.

The following table shows the development of total route length of government-owned railways in Australia, including Tasmania:

| Year | km | miles | Year | km | miles |
|---|---|---|---|---|---|
| 1860 | 340 | 211 | 1930 | 42 733 | 26 554 |
| 1870 | 1 501 | 933 | 1940 | 43 694 | 27 151 |
| 1880 | 5 467 | 3 397 | 1950 | 42 255 | 26 878 |
| 1890 | 14 579 | 9 059 | 1960 | 42 082 | 26 149 |
| 1900 | 20 126 | 12 506 | 1970 | 40 240 | 25 004 |
| 1910 | 24 880 | 15 460 | 1979 | 39 388 | 24 474 |
| 1920 | 37 204 | 23 118 | | | |

The Australian National Railways system (see p 120) includes routes in all the states and the Victorian system extends into New South Wales. The following table shows the route-km of each system at 30 June 1979.

| System | Gauge | | | Total |
|---|---|---|---|---|
| | 1 600 mm | 1 435 mm | 1 067 mm | |
| New South Wales (State Railway Authority) | — | 9 820[1] | — | 9 820 |
| Victoria | 5 859[2] | 325 | — | 6 184 |
| Queensland | — | 111[3] | 9 678 | 9 789 |
| South Australia | 142[4] | — | — | 142 |
| Western Australia | — | 1 377 | 4 393 | 5 770 |

| System | Gauge | | | Total |
|---|---|---|---|---|
| | 1 600 mm | 1 435 mm | 1 067 mm | |
| National (ANR) | 2 395⁴ | 2 610 | 2 678 | 7 683 |
| Australia total | 8 396 | 14 243 | 16 749 | 39 388 |

[1] Includes 456 km electrified route.
[2] Includes 328 km of 1600 mm gauge line operating in NSW: and 447 km electrified route.
[3] Operated by the State Rail Authority of NSW which is re-imbursed for the cost of operations.
[4] Since 1 March 1978 ANR has assumed responsibility for all South Australian railways except the 142 km of Adelaide metropolitan passenger railways operated by South Australian State Transport Authority—Rail Division.

Government railways rolling stock included in capital account; actual numbers, excluding jointly-owned stock, 30 June 1979, are as follows:

| | NSW | Vic | Qld | SA | WA | ANR | Australia |
|---|---|---|---|---|---|---|---|
| Locomotives: | | | | | | | |
| Diesel-electric | 485 | 266 | 455 | 2 | 194 | 293 | 1 695 |
| Electric | 39 | 35 | — | — | — | — | 74 |
| Other[1] | 20 | 41 | 77 | 4 | 21 | 40 | 203 |
| TOTAL | 544 | 342 | 532 | 6 | 215 | 333 | 1 972 |
| Coaching stock | 2 080 | 1 517 | 1 043 | 165 | 137 | 113 | 5 055 |
| Goods stock | 13 040 | 12 645 | 20 731 | — | 10 356 | 10 391 | 67 163 |
| Service stock | 1 978 | 1 181 | 2 361 | 14 | 482 | 1 176 | 7 192 |

[1] Includes non-passenger-carrying diesel power-vans and steam locomotives.

Train-kilometres (000s) on government-owned railway systems, 1978—9, revenue services only:

| | NSW | Vic | Qld | SA[1] | WA | ANR | Australia |
|---|---|---|---|---|---|---|---|
| Suburban passr. | 20 715 | 13 386 | 3 693 | 3 957 | 2 201 | — | 43 952 |
| Country passr. | 9 704 | 6 650 | 3 939 | — | 1 118 | 3 171 | 24 582 |
| Goods, inc. mixed | 25 203 | 10 820 | 24 469 | — | 8 749 | 9 746 | 78 986 |
| TOTAL | 55 622 | 30 856 | 32 100 | 3 957 | 12 068 | 12 918 | 147 520 |

|  | NSW | Vic | Qld | SA[1] | WA | ANR | Australia |
|---|---|---|---|---|---|---|---|
| Type of motive power, 000 km: |  |  |  |  |  |  |  |
| Diesel-elec. locos | 30 653 | 15 120 | 29 642 | 4 | 9 468 | 11 983 | 96 871 |
| Elec. and other locos inc. steam | 2 539 | 1 350 | 226 | 2 | 1 | — | 4 117 |
| Powered coaching stock | 22 430 | 14 386 | 2 233 | 3 950 | 2 599 | 934 | 46 532 |
| TOTAL | 55 622 | 30 856 | 32 100 | 3 957 | 12 068 | 12 918 | 147 520 |

[1] Figures for South Australia represent Adelaide suburban services only.

Passenger and freight traffic on government-owned railway systems in 1978–9, revenue services only, 000s train-kilometres:

The following table shows: Freight commodities carried on government-owned railway systems in 1978–9, 000 tonnes. Inter-system traffic included in total for each system over which it passes. South Australia and Tasmania included in Australian National Railways.

|  | NSW | Vic | Qld | WA | ANR | Australia |
|---|---|---|---|---|---|---|
| Grain | 3 260 | 2 884 | 1 816 | 3 109 | 1 093 | 12 162 |
| Other agricultural produce | 1 208 | 348 | 1 816 | 179 | 97 | 3 648 |
| Coal, coke and briquettes | 17 913 | 783 | 24 121 | 1 399 | 1 692 | 45 908 |
| Other minerals, sand, gravel | 2 939 | 745 | 3 949 | 10 680 | 1 653 | 19 966 |
| Iron and steel | 1 786 | 610 | [1] | — | 657 | 3 053 |
| Fertilisers | 271 | 672 | 122 | 479 | 484 | 2 028 |
| Cement | 425 | 774 | 139 | 68 | 464 | 1 870 |
| Timber | 94 | 180 | 113 | 210 | 821 | 1 418 |
| Containers | 2 724 | 831 | 759 | — | 1 067 | 5 381 |
| Livestock | 160 | 162 | 1 212 | 17 | 310 | 1 861 |
| All other commodities | 2 702 | 3 202 | 2 494 | 3 148 | 2 285 | 13 831 |

[1] Included in 'All other commodities'.

Passenger and freight traffic on government-owned railway systems in 1978–9, revenue services only, 000 train-kilometres:

| | NSW | Vic | Qld | SA | WA | ANR | Australia |
|---|---|---|---|---|---|---|---|
| Passenger journeys (000s):[1] | | | | | | | |
| Suburban | 179 079 | 89 258 | 25 850 | 70 526 | na | — | na |
| Country[2] | 3 670 | 4 065 | 1 425 | — | 234 | 677 | 10 071 |
| TOTAL | 182 749 | 93 323 | 27 275 | 70 526 | na | 677 | na |
| Passenger-km (000s): | | | | | | | |
| Suburban | na | 1 458 932 | na | na | na | | na |
| Country | na | 432 045 | na | na | 98 329 | 296 203 | na |
| TOTAL | na | 1 890 977 | na | na | na | 296 203 | na |
| Freight:[2] | | | | | | | |
| Tonnes carried (000s) | 33 482 | 11 190 | 36 542 | — | 19 288 | 10 623 | 111 125 |
| Net tonne-km (million) | 8 776.7 | 3 145.3 | 10 952.2 | — | 4 178.8 | 5 029.5 | 32 055.5 |

na – not available.
[1] Based on ticket sales making allowance for season tickets. Tickets at concessionary rates counted as full journeys.
[2] Inter-system traffic included in total for each system over which it passes.

## Net tonne-km of Freight on Government-owned Railway Systems, 1978–9

(South Australia and Tasmania included with ANR. Million tonne-km.)

| | NSW | Vic | Qld | WA | ANR | Australia |
|---|---|---|---|---|---|---|
| Grain | 1 231.3 | 829.8 [1] | | 939.7 | 188.1 [1] | |
| Other agricultural produce | 627.3 | 111.3 [1] | | 74.6 | 57.7 [1] | |
| Coal, coke and briquettes | 1 565.5 | 139.6 [1] | | 219.1 | 433.5 [1] | |
| Other minerals, sand, gravel | 581.3 | 130.1 [1] | | 1 444.2 | 381.4 [1] | |
| Iron and steel | 1 221.7 | 197.4 [1] | | — | 603.6 [1] | |
| Fertilisers | 166.6 | 168.4 [1] | | 184.8 | 163.5 [1] | |
| Cement | 141.5 | 115.3 [1] | | 29.4 | 66.0 [1] | |
| Timber | 92.8 | 59.9 [1] | | 69.1 | 168.2 [1] | |
| Containers | 1 522.0 | 342.4 [1] | | — | 845.8 [1] | |
| Livestock | 101.1 | 49.4 | 662.4 | 6.8 | 161.2 | 980.9 |
| All other commodities | 1 525.6 | 1 001.6 | 10 262.8 | 1 211.2 | 1 960.5 | 15 961.7 |
| TOTAL | 8 776.7 | 3 145.3 | 10 925.2 | 4 178.8 | 5 029.5 | 32 055.5 |

[1] Not available separately; included with 'All other commodities'.

## AUSTRALIAN NATIONAL RAILWAYS

The Australian National Railways Commission came into existence on 1 July 1975 to control the former Commonwealth Railways and also the Tasmanian and non-metropolitan South Australian Railways which were transferred to it on 1 March 1978. As the Commonwealth Railways its function was to operate lines connecting different states. Its earliest line was opened in 1879. The system comprises the following lines:

Trans-Australian Railway, Port Pirie (SA) to Kalgoorlie (WA), 1435 mm gauge, 1782 km (1107 miles), opened 1917;

Port Augusta–Whyalla branch (SA), 1435 mm gauge, 75 km (47 miles), opened 6 October 1972;

Central Australian Railway, Stirling North–Marree (SA), 1435 mm gauge, 350 km (217 miles), opened 1879 onwards;

Australian Capital Territory Railway, Canberra–Queanbeyan (on NSW Government system), 1435 mm gauge, 8 km (5 miles), opened 1914;

Tarcoola (SA) on Trans-Australian Railway–Alice Springs (opened 9 October 1980 as part of the North–South Continental Railway), 1435 mm gauge, 831 km (517 miles);

North Australian Railway (NT), Darwin–Larrimah, 1067 mm gauge, 503 km (312 miles) (no longer operating), opened 1889–1929;

Marree–Alice Springs (SA–NT) (closed 1 January 1981) 1067 mm gauge, 869 km (540 miles), opened 1929;

Tasmanian Region, 1067 mm gauge, 864 km (537 miles);

Former South Australian Government lines, 1600 mm gauge, 2395 km (1488 miles); 1435 mm gauge, 1871 km (1163 miles); 1067 mm gauge, 1536 km (954 miles).

## Development of Australian National, formerly Commonwealth, Railways

| Year | km | miles | Year | km | miles |
|------|------|------|------|------|------|
| 1880 | 105 | 65 | 1940 | 3 542 | 2 201 |
| 1890 | 917 | 570 | 1950 | 3 542 | 2 201 |
| 1900 | 1 004 | 624 | 1960 | 3 624 | 2 252 |
| 1910 | 1 004 | 624 | 1970 | 5 592 | 3 475 |
| 1920 | 2 792 | 1 735 | 1979 | 7 683 | 4 774 |
| 1930 | 3 451 | 2 145 | | | |

## STATE RAIL AUTHORITY OF NEW SOUTH WALES

Railways in New South Wales have been government-owned since before the earliest railway was opened, the 22.5 km (14 mile) long, 1435 mm gauge, line from Sydney to Parramatta, on 26 September 1855. The route length of the state railway system developed as follows:

| Year | km | miles | Year | km | miles |
|------|------|------|------|------|------|
| 1860 | 113 | 70 | 1890 | 3 511 | 2 182 |
| 1870 | 546 | 339 | 1900 | 4 524 | 2 811 |
| 1880 | 1 367 | 849 | 1910 | 5 863 | 3 643 |
| | | | 1920 | 8 071 | 5 015 |

| Year | km | miles | Year | km | miles |
|------|------|------|------|------|------|
| 1930 | 9 614 | 5 974 | 1960 | 9 830 | 6 108 |
| 1940 | 9 883 | 6 141 | 1970 | 9 755 | 6 061 |
| 1950 | 9 836 | 6 112 | 1980 | 9 773 | 6 073 |

The route length reached its maximum of 9918 km (6163 miles) in 1934.

In October 1972 the Public Transport Commission of New South Wales was established and it took over responsibility for the NSW Government Railways system and omnibus services which were previously operated by the Commissioner for Railways and the Commissioner for Public Transport.

On 1 July 1980 under the Transport Authorities Act 1980, the Public Transport Commission of New South Wales was dissolved and replaced by two separate organisations: the Urban Transit Authority (UTA) and the State Rail Authority (SRA), both under control of the Minister for Transport. Also the Railway Workshops Board was established as a subsidiary of the SRA.

The UTA is responsible for the co-ordination of bus, rail, ferry and taxi services in the urban and inter-urban areas of Sydney, Newcastle and Wollongong.

The SRA is responsible for all passenger and freight rail services and for providing inter-urban passenger rail services in consultation with the UTA.

The total length of railways open for traffic in New South Wales at 30 June 1980 was 10 218 km (6348 miles). It comprised 9773 km (6073 miles) owned by the NSW Government; a line of 6 km (3.7 miles) from St Mary's to Ropes Creek; and one of 47 km (29 miles) from Broken Hill to Cockburn (SA) owned by the Commonwealth Government; 324 km (201 miles) of railways owned by the Victoria Government in the Riverina district; and 68 km (42 miles) of privately-owned railways available for general traffic.

## Length of Route, SRA, at 30 June 1980

| | km | miles |
|------|------|------|
| Single track | 8 553 | 5 315 |
| Double track | 1 114 | 692 |
| Three or more tracks | 106 | 66 |
| Sidings and crossovers | 2 553 | 1 586 |

|                          | km     | miles  |
|--------------------------|--------|--------|
| Total single-track length | 13 787 | 8 567 |
| Electrified track         | 456    | 283   |

In Sydney a double-track electric railway, mostly underground, surrounds the city. The eastern section, Central to St James, 1.5 km (1 mile), was completed in 1926; the western section, Central to Wynyard, 2.4 km (1.5 miles), in 1932. With the opening of Sydney Harbour Bridge in 1932 services on the main western, southern and northern lines were connected with the North Sydney line via Wynyard. The link between St James and Wynyard including a station at Circular Quay was opened in 1956.

**Traffic on New South Wales State Railways, 1979–80**

| *Passenger journeys* | *No* |
|---|---|
| | 208 821 000 |
| (Including Sydney and Newcastle urban services | 204 961) |

| *Freight commodities, 000 tonnes* | |
|---|---|
| Coal | 20 068 |
| Wheat | 6 056 |
| Iron and steel | 2 127 |
| Containers | 3 025 |
| Other | 8 410 |
| TOTAL | 39 686 |

| *Rolling stock* | *No* |
|---|---|
| Locomotives: | |
| Steam | — |
| Diesel-electric main-line | 218 |
| Diesel shunters | 81 |
| Diesel power vans | 4 |
| Electric | 39 |

| Coaching stock[1] | No | Passenger capacity |
|---|---|---|
| Loco-hauled | | |
| Southern Aurora[2] | | |
| Sleeping carriages | 26 | 516 |
| Other coaching stock | 15 | — |
| Other | | |
| Sleeping carriages | 76 | 1 494 |
| Sitting carriages | 663 | 27 954 |
| Other coaching stock | 223 | — |
| Rail-motor services | 106 | 4 720 |
| Multiple-unit trains, diesel | 36 | 1 245 |
| Diesel trains | 13 | 414 |
| Budd sets | 5 | 314 |
| Suburban electric | | |
| Single-deck carriages | 857 | 60 245 |
| Double-deck carriages | 247 | 30 558 |
| Parcel vans | 8 | — |
| Inter-urban electric | | |
| Single-deck carriages | 80 | 4 640 |
| Double-deck carriages | 16 | 1 520 |
| Diesel rail-cars | 8 | 402 |

| Goods stock | No | Capacity, tonnes |
|---|---|---|
| Open wagons | 8 670 | 201 478 |
| Flat wagons | 1 335 | 59 899 |
| Bolster wagons | 220 | 9 226 |
| Wheat wagons | 1 303 | 48 891 |
| Livestock wagons | 864 | 9 622 |
| Coal wagons | 1 985 | 79 180 |
| Louvred vans | 1 184 | 46 988 |
| Refrigerator vans | 524 | 10 200 |
| Brake vans | 680 | — |
| Other | 1 041 | 36 442 |
| Service stock | 1 961 | — |

[1] Excludes carriages of the Indian Pacific Trans-Continental Service (34 at June 1975) operated jointly by ANR, SRA and WA Government Railways.
[2] 'Southern Aurora' coaching stock is owned jointly by SRA and Victorian Government Railways.

## VICTORIAN RAILWAYS (VicRail)

Victoria has the honour of introducing steam railways to Australia. The first line, 4 km (2½ miles) long, from Flinders Street, Melbourne, to Sandridge, was opened on 12 September 1854. A gauge of 1600 mm (5 ft 3 in) was used, the result of employing an Irish engineer, F. W. Shields, who adopted the gauge standard in Ireland. The gauge was a compromise between the standard 1435 mm (4 ft 8½ in) gauge of the Dublin & Kingstown Railway (1834) and the 1880 mm (6 ft 2 in) of the Belfast–Lisburn line (1839).

### Development of Victorian Railways

| Year | km | miles | Year | km | miles |
|------|------|-------|------|------|-------|
| 1860 | 137 | 85 | 1930 | 7 584 | 4 713 |
| 1870 | 409 | 254 | 1940 | 7 659 | 4 759 |
| 1880 | 1 930 | 1 199 | 1950 | 7 543 | 4 687 |
| 1890 | 3 975 | 2 470 | 1960 | 6 904 | 4 290 |
| 1900 | 5 179 | 3 218 | 1970 | 6 704 | 4 166 |
| 1910 | 5 618 | 3 491 | 1980 | 6 184 | 3 843 |
| 1920 | 6 782 | 4 214 | | | |

The 1980 total of 6184 km includes 5313 km (3301 miles) of single-track route, 731 km (454 miles) of double track and 140 km (87 miles) of multiple track. 328 km (204 miles) of Victorian Railways lines operates over the border into New South Wales.

In 1978–9 Victorian Railways salaried staff numbered 5388 and wages staff 17 361, a total of 22 749 persons.

*Rolling stock in service at 30 June 1980*

| Locomotives: | steam | 10 |
|---|---|---|
| | electric | 35 |
| | diesel electric | 257 |
| | other[1] | 88 |
| TOTAL | | 400 |

| Passenger coaches: | electric suburban | 1 038 |
|---|---|---|
| | other[2] | 469 |
| TOTAL | | 1 507 |

| | |
|---|---|
| Goods stock[3] | 12 165 |
| Service stock | 1 154 |

[1] Other locomotives comprise diesel-hydraulic locomotives, cranes, rail-motor diesel power units, and non-passenger-carrying tractors.
[2] Passenger coaches owned jointly with NSW and SA have been included.
[3] Including parcels and brake vans, display cars and standard-gauge stock.

*Victorian Railways traffic, 1979–80*

| | |
|---|---|
| Train-km: country passenger, 000s | 6 208 |
| suburban passenger, 000s | 13 174 |
| goods, 000s | 11 413 |
| TOTAL | 30 795 |
| Passenger journeys: country, 000s | 3 664 |
| suburban, 000s | 85 247 |
| TOTAL, 000s | 88 911 |
| Goods and livestock carried, 000 tonnes | 13 453 |

Goods and livestock traffic by commodities; in tonnes and tonne-km, 1979–80 (figures for 1978–9 in brackets) are as follows:

| Commodities | 000 tonnes | | Tonne-km | |
|---|---|---|---|---|
| Grain: barley | 548 | (471) | 147 387 | (124 599) |
| wheat | 4 164 | (4 164) | 1 309 886 | (661 463) |
| other | 349 | (233) | 70 321 | (43 735) |
| Flour | 59 | (77) | 14 850 | (17 196) |
| Stockfood and fodder | 35 | (35) | 9 194 | (8 407) |
| Fruit: fresh | 76 | (78) | 26 491 | (28 469) |
| dried | 45 | (53) | 24 650 | (29 160) |
| Beverages | 143 | (147) | 33 976 | (35 082) |
| Dairy produce | 13 | (14) | 2 872 | (3 620) |
| Milk: condensed, powdered, etc | 47 | (60) | 9 010 | (10 778) |
| Manures | 631 | (671) | 160 240 | (168 449) |
| Solid fuels | 783 | (783) | 139 537 | (139 606) |
| Cement | 718 | (774) | 118 245 | (115 338) |
| Mining and quarry products | 867 | (745) | 146 558 | (130 052) |
| Tinplate | 26 | (21) | 10 654 | (7 339) |

| Commodities | 000 tonnes | | Tonne-km | |
|---|---|---|---|---|
| Iron, steel and metals, unfabricated | 749 | (609) | 250 419 | (197 447) |
| Motor cars and accessories | 165 | (173) | 39 773 | (44 733) |
| Petroleum products | 341 | (388) | 109 976 | (120 892) |
| Paper products | 194 | (193) | 70 980 | (72 800) |
| Pipes | 54 | (57) | 14 361 | (15 323) |
| Timber | 187 | (180) | 65 522 | (59 918) |
| Wool | 92 | (100) | 24 157 | (25 766) |
| All other goods | 3 039 | (2 980) | 1 047 157 | (1 035 757) |
| TOTAL goods | 13 325 | (13 006) | 3 846 216 | (3 095 929) |
| TOTAL livestock | 128 | (162) | 41 578 | (49 376) |
| TOTAL goods and livestock | 13 453 | (11 190) | 3 887 794 | (3 145 305) |

Unlike many major cities, Melbourne, the capital of Victoria, has maintained and developed its electric trams which operate over 224 km (138 miles) of route, and in 1980—1 carried 121 000 000 passengers. The Tramways Board employs 4600 persons.

## QUEENSLAND RAILWAYS

For economy the Queensland Government adopted a gauge of 1067 mm (3 ft 6 in) for the first railway in the colony, opened in July 1865 between Ipswich and Grandchester, 33 km (22½ miles). Queensland was the first railway authority in the world to adopt a sub-standard gauge for main lines.

### Development of Queensland Railways

| Year | km | miles | Year | km | miles |
|---|---|---|---|---|---|
| 1870 | 333 | 207 | 1930 | 10 327 | 6 417 |
| 1880 | 1 028 | 639 | 1940 | 10 407 | 6 467 |
| 1890 | 3 399 | 2 112 | 1950 | 10 398 | 6 461 |
| 1900 | 4 508 | 2 801 | 1960 | 10 151 | 6 308 |
| 1910 | 5 892 | 3 661 | 1970 | 9 406 | 5 845 |
| 1920 | 9 101 | 5 655 | 1981 | 9 932 | 6 171 |

Of the total at 30 June 1981 9821 km (6102 miles) was 1067 mm gauge and

111 km (69 miles) was 1435 mm gauge in connection with the NSW system and was operated by the NSW Railways Commissioner. This interstate uniform-gauge line was begun in 1926 and opened in 1930.

*Rolling stock at 30 June 1981:*

| | |
|---|---:|
| Diesel locomotives: electric | 482 |
|                  hydraulic | 73 |
|                  mechanical | 4 |
| TOTAL | 559 |
| Passenger coaches | 905 |
| Electric multiple-unit cars (19 × 3) | 57 |
| Rail-motors, trailers, etc | 68 |
| Brake vans | 186 |
| Wagons | 23 747 |

Since the introduction of diesel-electric locomotives the average gross load of goods and livestock trains on the 1067 mm gauge has risen from 317 tonnes in 1953–4 to 1054 tonnes in 1980–1.

Important items of freight are coal and coke of which 29 742 357 tonnes were carried in 1980–1, an increase of 4 105 319 tonnes on 1979–80; wool 20 924 tonnes, a fall of 6926 tonnes on 1979–80; and livestock 619 000 tonnes, a fall of 224 580 tonnes on 1979–80.

For operational purposes the Queensland Railways system is divided into three divisions: Southern, Central and Northern. The Uniform Gauge Railway from South Brisbane to Kyogle on the border of New South Wales is included with the Southern Division.

## Divisional Operations 1980–1

| Particulars | Southern Division | Central Division | Northern Division | Total |
|---|---:|---:|---:|---:|
| Lines open, km | 3 721 | 3 169 | 3 042 | 9 932 |
| Revenue train-km, 000s | 13 901 | 10 802 | 6 580 | 31 282 |
| Train-km per km of line open | 3 735 | 3 409 | 2 163 | 3 150 |
| Passenger traffic: | | | | |
| Train-km, country, 000s | | | | 4 097 |
|            suburban, 000s | | | | 4 165 |
| TOTAL, 000s | | | | 8 262 |

| Particulars | Southern Division | Central Division | Northern Division | Total |
|---|---|---|---|---|
| Passengers carried: | | | | |
| country, 000s | | | | 1 544 |
| suburban, 000s | | | | 30 330 |
| TOTAL, 000s | 31 478 | 80 | 315 | 31 873 |
| Goods traffic: | | | | |
| Train-km, 000s | | | | 23 020 |
| Freight carried, 000 tonnes | | | | 41 504 |
| Minerals, inc. coal, 000 tonnes | 400 | 29 298 | 4 400 | 34 098 |
| Agricultural produce, 000 tonnes | 995 | 994 | 1 125 | 3 113 |
| Other goods, 000 tonnes | 2 887 | 425 | 362 | 3 674 |
| Livestock, 000 tonnes | 137 | 218 | 265 | 619 |
| Average length of haul, km | | | | 286 |
| Average gross load of goods trains[1] tonnes | | | | 1 054 |

[1] Excluding the Normanton Railway and the Innisfail and Mourilyan Tramways. Over a period of five years passenger traffic has declined by about 7 per cent, but tonnage of freight carried has increased by 25 per cent. The biggest increase is in minerals including coal, 35.7 per cent.

## SOUTH AUSTRALIAN RAILWAYS

As in the neighbouring state of Victoria, South Australia adopted the 1600 mm (5 ft 3 in) gauge for its first railway from Adelaide to Port Adelaide, 12 km (7½ miles), opened on 21 April 1856. It was built and worked by the South Australian Government. Although the 1600 mm gauge was adopted as standard, a considerable length of secondary route was built to 1067 mm gauge and its position between New South Wales and Western Australia has resulted in South Australia being crossed by the 1435 mm gauge transcontinental line. Thus South Australia is the only state in Australia to have all three gauges, and at Peterborough on the Port Pirie–Broken Hill section and at Gladstone, north of Adelaide, there is triple-gauge track. Out of a total of 5944 km (3693 miles) of route, 2537 km (1576 miles) is 1600 mm gauge; 1871 km (1163 miles) is 1435 mm gauge; and 1536 km (954 miles) is 1067 mm gauge.

On 1 March 1978 the whole of the South Australian Government Railways was handed over to the Australian National Railways Commission except for the Adelaide suburban network of 143 km (89 miles), shown in the following table.

## Development of South Australian Government Railways

| Year | km | miles | Year | km | miles |
|------|------|-------|------|------|-------|
| 1860 | 90 | 56 | 1930 | 4 080 | 2 535 |
| 1870 | 214 | 133 | 1940 | 4 115 | 1 557 |
| 1880 | 912 | 567 | 1950 | 4 107 | 2 552 |
| 1890 | 1 910 | 1 187 | 1960 | 4 076 | 2 533 |
| 1900 | 2 026 | 1 259 | 1970 | 3 884 | 2 413 |
| 1910 | 2 309 | 1 435 | 1980 | 143 | 89 |
| 1920 | 3 754 | 2 333 | | | |

Triple-gauge track at the south end of Gladstone Yard, South Australia, on wheat silo discharge tracks, in 1973; 1067 mm (3 ft 6 in), 1435 mm (4 ft 8½ in) and 1600 mm (5 ft 3 in). (A. Grunbach)

**Development of Traffic on South Australian Government Railways 1856–1976**

| Year | Passengers carried (000s) | Goods carried (000 tonnes) |
|---|---|---|
| 1856 | 248 | 32 |
| 1866 | 425 | 145 |
| 1876 | 1 400 | 387 |
| 1885–6 | 3 962 | 779 |
| 1895–6 | 5 436 | 1 057 |
| 1905–6 | 10 715 | 1 732 |
| 1915–16 | 20 513 | 2 397 |
| 1925–6 | 25 752 | 3 563 |
| 1935–6 | 17 431 | 2 482 |
| 1945–6 | 23 119 | 2 997 |
| 1955–6 | 16 434 | 4 436 |
| 1965–6 | 15 511 | 4 823 |
| 1975–6 | 12 672 | 6 184 |
| 1976–7 | 12 866 | 6 442 |

## WESTERN AUSTRALIAN GOVERNMENT RAILWAYS

The first railway in the colony was a private timber-carrying line from Yoganup to Luckeville built to a gauge of 1067 mm (3 ft 6 in), 19 km (12 miles), opened on 6 June 1871. It was worked by horses until August when the locomotive *Ballerat* arrived from Ballerat, Victoria, where it was built. In 1879 the Geraldton–Northampton line was opened, 55 km (34 miles). The first railway to Perth, from Fremantle, was opened in 1881. These early lines were acquired by the Western Australian Government in 1896.

Railways in Western Australia developed as follows:

| Year | km | miles | Year | km | miles |
|---|---|---|---|---|---|
| 1880 | 53 | 33 | 1910 | 3 452 | 2 145 |
| 1890 | 303 | 188 | 1920 | 5 696 | 3 539 |
| 1900 | 2 181 | 1 355 | 1930 | 6 616 | 4 111 |

| Year | km | miles | Year | km | miles |
|------|------|-------|------|------|-------|
| 1940 | 7 050 | 4 381 | 1970 | 6 835 | 4 247 |
| 1950 | 6 842 | 4 252 | 1980 | 6 504 | 4 041 |
| 1960 | 6 630 | 4 120 | | | |

Of the 6504 km open at 30 June 1980, 5773 km (3587 miles) were owned by the state government and operated by the Western Australian Government Commission; 731 km (454 miles) were owned by the Commonwealth Government and operated by Australian National Railways Commission. The 5773 km of government-owned railway was made up as follows: 1067 mm gauge, 4396 km (2732 miles); 1435 mm gauge, 1229 km (764 miles); dual gauge, 148 km (92 miles).

The following private railways are used for the transport of iron ore:

| | Gauge, mm | km | miles | Opened |
|---|------|------|-------|--------|
| Shay Gap–Port Hedland | 1 435 | 180 | 112 | 23.5.1966 |
| Hammersley Iron Ore Railways Paraburdoo–Dampier | 1 435 | 382 | 237 | 1.7.1966 |
| Koolyanobbing–Kwinana[1] | 1 435 | 490 | 304 | 10.4.1967 |
| Northam–Wundowie[2] | 1 067 | 33 | 21 | 10.4.1967 |
| Mount Newman Railroad Newman–Port Hedland | 1 435 | 430 | 267 | 18.1.1969 |
| Robe River Railroad Pannawonica–Cape Lambert | 1 435 | 167 | 104 | 6.7.1972 |

[1] Part of WA Government system open for general and passenger traffic.
[2] Part of WA Government system used only for transport of iron ore from Koolyanobbing to the charcoal iron and steel industry at Wundowie.

In 1979–80 these railways carried 89 700 000 tonnes of ore. At 30 June 1980 they operated 130 locomotives and 5618 ore wagons.

The standard-gauge Trans-Australian Railway was opened from Port Augusta to Kalgoorlie, 1693 km (1052 miles), on 22 October 1917. At Kalgoorlie it connected with the Western Australian Government 1067 mm system. With the conversion of the Kalgoorlie–Perth section in Western Australia and of the section from Port Pirie to Broken Hill in South Australia from 1067 mm to standard gauge, completed on 29 November 1969, a through route entirely on standard gauge was opened from Perth to Sydney, 3960 km (2461 miles).

### Rolling Stock of Western Australian Government Railways at 30 June 1980

|  | 1 067 mm gauge | 1 435 mm gauge |
|---|---|---|
| Locomotives: steam | 2 | — |
| diesel | 164 | 44 |
| TOTAL | 166 | 44 |
| Coaching stock | 131 | 9 |
| Goods stock[1] | 8 778 | 1 278 |
| Service stock[2] | 390 | 83 |

[1] Includes brake vans, goods wagons, livestock wagons, mineral wagons etc.
[2] Includes ballast wagons, workmen's vans, ash disposal wagons, water tanks, etc.

*Operations 1979–80 (figures for 1974–5 in brackets):*

| | | |
|---|---|---|
| Train-km, revenue and non revenue | 12 486 | (13 812) |
| Passenger journeys: suburban,[1] 000s | 7 132 | (10 006) |
| country, 000s | 418 | (469) |
| TOTAL, 000s | 7 550 | (10 474) |
| Tonnes of freight, 000s: | | |
| Paying goods and livestock | 21 388 | (16 348) |
| Departmental[2] | 549 | (222) |
| TOTAL | 21 937 | (16 570) |
| Tonne-km: | | |
| Paying goods and livestock | 4 730 671 | (4 269 270) |
| Departmental | 69 438 | (41 445) |
| TOTAL | 4 800 109 | (4 310 715) |

[1] Responsibility for the financial and policy direction of the suburban railways passed to the Metropolitan (Perth) Passenger Transport Trust from 1 July 1974.
[2] Departmental freight comprises mainly oil, ballast, timber and rails.

## TASMANIA

Apart from a wooden railway built in 1836, the first railway in Tasmania, between Launceston and Deloraine, 72 km (45 miles), was opened in 1871 with a gauge of 1600 mm as in South Australia and Victoria. It was taken over by the government in 1872 as was the later Launceston (Western Junction)–Hobart line, 196 km (122 miles), opened in 1876. These lines were converted to 1067 mm gauge in 1888, and this became the standard gauge in Tasmania. The first line built to 1067 mm gauge was opened in 1885.

Development of government-owned railways in Tasmania was as follows:

| Year | km | miles | Year | km | miles |
|------|------|-----|------|-------|-----|
| 1880 | 72 | 45 | 1940 | 1 036 | 644 |
| 1890 | 602 | 374 | 1950 | 987 | 613 |
| 1900 | 705 | 438 | 1960 | 866 | 538 |
| 1910 | 756 | 470 | 1970 | 805 | 500 |
| 1920 | 1 012 | 629 | 1977 | 849 | 528 |
| 1930 | 1 093 | 679 | | | |

On 1 July 1975 the Tasmanian railways were transferred to the Australian National Railways Commission. Recent figures for Tasmanian rolling stock as distinct from the remainder of ANR are not available. At the time of the transfer there were: 3 steam locos; 44 diesel-electric locos; 2 diesel-hydraulic locos; 19 diesel-shunters; 13 diesel railcars and 5 trailers; 43 passenger coaches; 2029 freight wagons.

*Operations on Tasmanian Railways, 1976–7:*

| | |
|---|---|
| Revenue train-km, 000s | 1 667 |
| Passenger journeys, 000s | 140[1] |
| Goods and livestock carried | 1 644 |

[1] The Hobart suburban rail passenger service ended on 31 December 1974.

Sources
*Australia Year Book* No 66 1982 pp 493–9
*New South Wales Year Books* 1976 pp 301–13, 1982 pp 371–6
*Victoria Year Book* 1982 pp 511–17
*Queensland Year Book* 1982 pp 229–33
*Western Australian Year Book* 1982 pp 461–5
*Tasmania Year Book* 1979 pp 292–5

# 9 Railways of the USSR (SZD)

Sovetski Zhelezno-Dorozhni (SZD)
'Soviet Metal Roadway'

The first railway in the USSR was the St Petersburg & Pavlovsk Railway, built to a gauge of 1829 mm (6 ft). The first portion, Pavlovsk to Tsarske Selo, was opened to horse traction on 9 October 1836. The entire railway was opened on 30 October 1837.

The 'Russian standard gauge' of 1524 mm (5 ft 0 in) was established by George Washington Whistler (qv), the American engineer who laid out the Moscow & St Petersburg Railway in 1843. He adopted this gauge because it was then the standard in his native Southern States. The 650 km (404 miles) railway, on the order of the Tsar, was laid out in an almost dead straight line. It was opened throughout on 1 November 1851. While, in the USA, the 5 ft, 5 ft 6 in and 6 ft gauge lines were converted to standard (1435 mm [4 ft 8½ in]) during the 1870s and 80s, in Russia the 5 ft gauge was adopted as the standard, and it was extended as follows:

| Year | km | miles | Year | km | miles |
|------|------|-------|------|--------|--------|
| 1840 | 27 | 17 | 1910 | 55 173 | 34 284 |
| 1850 | 174 | 108 | 1920 | 71 595 | 44 488 |
| 1860 | 1 077 | 669 | 1930 | 77 860 | 48 381 |
| 1870 | 8 428 | 5 237 | 1940 | 106 100 | 65 929 |
| 1880 | 17 709 | 11 004 | 1950 | 116 875 | 72 625 |
| 1890 | 23 419 | 14 552 | 1960 | 125 789 | 78 164 |
| 1900 | 44 491 | 27 646 | 1972 | 136 294 | 84 689 |
|      |      |       | 1982 | 141 846 | 88 139 |

With a total route length of 145 977 km (90 705 miles) in the USSR, Mongolia and Eastern Europe, compared with standard gauge route length of 235 210 km (146 152 miles) in the remainder of Europe there is now no question of conversion. Inconvenience is limited to changes of bogies and couplings at frontier stations, carried out with great speed and efficiency.

In line with modern practice the gauge is being narrowed to 1520 mm (4 ft 11⅞ in) with vertical rails (not inclined inwards). The standard was changed on 1 January 1972.

Of the total route length of 139 200 km (86 495 miles) of Russian gauge route 43 700 km (27 154 miles), or 31.4 per cent, is electrified at 3000 V dc or 25 kV 50 Hz. Further electrification, mostly at 25 kV 50 Hz, is proceeding rapidly. The total route length of 141 846 km (88 139 miles) includes 2571 km (1598 miles) of narrow-gauge line 600 mm (1 ft 11⅝ in) gauge to 1 metre gauge and 75 km (47 miles) of 1435 mm (4 ft 8½ in) gauge. Traffic has grown as follows:

|                               | 1913 | 1940  | 1965    | 1970    | 1980    |
|-------------------------------|------|-------|---------|---------|---------|
| Passengers, millions          | 249  | 1 377 | 2 301   | 2 390   | 3 566   |
| Freight (000 million tonne-km)| 76.4 | 420.7 | 1 950.2 | 2 494.6 | 3 739.9 |

Freight, by commodities, carried in 1980 (million tonnes):

| Coal                          | 732 |
|-------------------------------|-----|
| Coke                          | 34  |
| Oil products                  | 423 |
| Ferrous metals                | 192 |
| Timber                        | 147 |
| Grain                         | 135 |
| Ores                          | 316 |
| Mineral construction materials| 957 |
| Mineral fertilisers           | 116 |
| Other                         | 678 |

Each year Soviet Railways transport over 200 million tonnes of agricultural freight, about two thirds of which is grain. About 20 million tonnes of potatoes, vegetables, beets and fruits are moved only 50 km or less by rail.

Soviet Railways employ about 2 196 000 persons.

Locomotives used on 25 kV 50 Hz lines include the VL80T of 6520 kW (8743 hp); the VL80R of 6250 kW (8381 hp); on 3000 V dc lines the WL10 of 5200 kW (6973 hp); and the triple-unit VL11 of 7850 kW (10 526 hp).

The Trans-Siberian Railway, Moscow to Vladivostock, 9297 km (5777 miles) was opened in sections. The first goods train reached Irkutsk,

Yaroslavski Station, Moscow, terminus of the Trans-Siberian Railway, 28 May 1981. (John Marshall)

Circum Baikal section of the Trans-Siberian Railway, opened in 1904. (John Marshall)

5191 km (3225 miles) from Moscow, on 27 August 1898. By ferry across Lake Baikal and via the Chinese Eastern Railway across Manchuria, through communication was established on 3 November 1901. The Circum Baikal line round the south of the lake was opened on 25 September 1904. The 1931 km (1200 mile) Amur line, entirely on Russian soil, was built between 1908 and 1916.

The Baikal–Amur northern main line, 3145 km (1954 miles), begun in 1938, is now nearing completion. The Kunerma–Krasnoiarsk section was opened in May 1982. Its construction involved 380 million cubic metres (497 million cubic yards) of earthwork including 200 million cubic metres of hard rock or permafrost ground. There are nine tunnels totalling 32 km (20 miles), 138 large bridges or viaducts and 3762 smaller bridges and culverts. The largest bridges at present completed are across the Lena, 500 m; Amur, 1500 m; and Zeya, 1100 m. Of the longest tunnels, three: Baikal, 6.7 km (4 miles 287 yd); Nagorny, 1.3 km (1422 yd); and Dusse-Alin, 1.8 km (1 mile 208 yd) are finished. Of the longest tunnel, North Mui, 15.4 km (9 miles 1000 yd), 4.6 km (2 miles 1510 yd) are completed, and the Kodar tunnel, 2.1 km (1 mile 426 yd) is started. These lengths are to the nearest 100 m, so the yards are only approximate.

The construction of more than 1200 km (746 miles) of this railway presented numerous unique problems. For nine months of each year snow falls often to depths of 2 m. Much of the ground is permanently frozen to depths of 5 to 300 m. Temperatures range from −58°C to 36°C (−74°F to 97°F); even at this temperature the permafrost ground thaws down to only 1 to 1.5 m (3 to 5 ft). Care has been taken to preserve the natural conditions maintained by the permafrost area. There is high earthquake activity, sometimes up to 6, 8 and 9 on the Richter scale; from 1979 to 82 there were 4000 earthquakes in the area. For 750 km (466 miles) from the western end the railway crosses high mountain ranges: the Baikal, North Mui, Udokan, and Stanovoy. Other construction difficulties were caused by thermal karsts (eroded limestone liable to sudden collapse), heaving ground, talus (scree slopes), areas threatened by avalanches and rock slides, and areas of saturated bog. Many bridges and buildings are supported on piles, some driven to depths as great as 28 m (92 ft). Information such as this makes it understandable why construction is taking so long.

Practically all excavation and track laying is by mechanical means. Track lies on a bed of sand 200 mm (8 in) thick and rock ballast 250 mm (10 in) deep. Rails of 65 kg/m (131 lb/yd) are in 25 m (82 ft) lengths laid on timber sleepers 46 per length, 1840 per km. The railway will open up vast mineral resources and is expected to generate employment for 40 000 staff bringing yet more problems, such as water supply and sewage disposal. All buildings must be highly insulated and triple-glazed to make human life possible in this inhospitable region.

In the mountain section electric traction at 25 kV will be used, with thyristor-controlled locomotives of class VL80R of 6520 kW, fitted with regenerative braking. Tests are being carried out with 8-axle VL84 class locomotive of 7600 kW.

To increase line capacity, SZD has double-tracked a total of 1244 km (773 miles) of route since 1981, as follows.

|  | km | miles |
| --- | --- | --- |
| Taishet−Krestovaya | 235 | 146 |
| Kandagach−Saksaulskaya | 287 | 178 |
| Tselinograd−Kockchetav | 160 | 99 |
| Mezhdurechensk−Abakan | 109 | 68 |
| Bui−Svecha | 152 | 94 |
| Alma-Ata−Chu | 123 | 76 |
| Kockchetav−Utyag | 178 | 111 |

Electrification of the Trans-Siberian Railway, partly on 3000 V dc and more recently on 25 kV 50 Hz, had reached Karimskaya, 6284 km (3905 miles) from Moscow, by 1980. By 1990 SZD hopes to have electrified the entire Trans-Siberian Railway.

# 10 Railways of China

The first railway in China was a 762 mm (2 ft 6 in) gauge line opened in 1876 from Shanghai to Woosung, about 32 km (20 miles). It was operated by two small 0−6−0 saddle tanks built by Ransomes & Rapier of Ipswich, England. The engineer was John Dixon (1835−91), a nephew of John Dixon of the Stockton & Darlington Railway. The Chinese were hostile and suspicious and, following a fatal accident, as soon as the redemption money was paid, in October 1877, the whole railway was dismantled and dumped in Taiwan (Formosa).

The first permanent railway in China was the standard-gauge

Chinese men at work in Shamulata Tunnel on the Chengtu−Kunming Railway, an example of the enormous difficulties in the construction of this line. (Chinese People's Republic Railways)

Tongshan–Hsukuchuang line opened in 1880, extended to Lutai in 1886 and to Tientsin in 1888. It now forms part of the Beijing (Peking)–Shen Yang (Mukden) section. Steam traction was introduced in 1883.

Railway development in China continued on a piecemeal basis with unconnected lines, some badly constructed, all over the vast country, with gaps at wide rivers crossed by unreliable ferries. By the time of the Japanese invasion in 1935 the total route length was about 20 000 km (12 400 miles). Under the government of the time the Chinese railways were totally unable to cope with the transport demands of war.

It was not until the Chinese People's Republic was established in 1949 that real progress was made. At that time only 11 000 km (6800 miles) of route were usable. Since then an average of about 800 km (500 miles), increasing to 1000 km (600 miles) have been built annually, with plans to add another 20 000 km by the end of the century. Older lines are being modernised, sinuous single lines are being completely rebuilt into straight double-track routes, vast rivers have been bridged, high-speed main lines have been built through some of the most difficult mountain terrain in the world, and a railway is even being built into Tibet at altitudes greater than those of railways in the Andes, all carried out entirely by the Chinese themselves.

## New Trunk Lines

| Name | Between | Opened | km | miles |
|------|---------|--------|-----|-------|
| Hunan–Guangxi | Hengyan–Pingxiang | 1952 | 1 013 | 629 |
| Chengdu–Chongqing | | 1953 | 504 | 313 |
| Tianshui–Lanzhou | | 1954 | 348 | 216 |
| Baoji–Chengdu | | 1957 | 669 | 416 |
| Baotou–Lanzhou | | 1958 | 979 | 608 |
| Yingtan–Xiamen | | 1958 | 694 | 431 |
| Lanzhou–Qinghai | Lanzhou–Haiyan | 1960 | 313 | 194 |
| Lanzhou–Xinjiang | Lanzhou–Urumqi | 1962 | 1 892 | 1 175 |
| Sichuan–Guizhou | Chongqing–Guiyang | 1965 | 463 | 288 |
| Guiyang–Kunming | | 1966 | 643 | 400 |
| Chengdu–Kunming | | 1970 | 1 100 | 684 |
| Jiaozuo–Zhicheng | | 1970 | 772 | 480 |
| Hunan–Guizhou | Zhuzhou–Guiyang | 1972 | 902 | 560 |
| Xiangfan–Chongqing | | 1978 | 951 | 591 |
| Zhicheng–Liuzhou | | 1978 | 885 | 550 |
| Beijing–Tongliao | | 1979 | 870 | 541 |

One of the latest lines to be completed, the 551 km (342 mile) Wuhu–Guixi line linking the provinces of Anhui and Jiangxi, was opened on 1 October 1982. It passes through the heart of the Huang Shan mountain range and it fills a major north–south gap in the eastern part of the railway network. On the line from Quinghai Province into Tibet the first 835 km (519 miles) from Xining to Golmud was opened on 1 October 1979. Passenger trains reached Golmud on 14 January 1982.

On 1 January 1983 a new railway was opened from Zhicheng in Hubei Province to Liuzhou in the Guangxi Zhuang Autonomous Region in the south, 885 km (550 miles) long. It has 396 tunnels totalling 172.3 km (107 miles), and 476 bridges totalling 52.25 km (32.5 miles).

The development of Chinese railways, all 1435 mm (4 ft 8½ in) gauge, was as follows:

| Year | km | miles | Year | km | miles |
|------|------|------|------|------|------|
| 1890 | 201 | 125 | 1950 | 29 294 | 18 203 |
| 1900 | 2 346 | 1 458 | 1960 | 31 381 | 19 500 |
| 1910 | 3 442 | 2 139 | 1972 | 35 003 | 21 750 |
| 1920 | 1 119 | 6 952 | 1982 | 50 000 | 31 000[1] |
| 1930 | 19 001 | 11 807 | | | |
| 1940 | na | na | | | |

na – not available; [1] approximate

## Permanent Way

Work is now in progress in replacing carbon-steel rails by medium manganese steel, increasing the life expectancy by 26 per cent. Since 1978 rails of 60 kg/m (120 lb/yd) have been used on lines with high traffic density. The average rail weight has been increased to 50 kg/m (100 lb/yd). About 7000 km (4350 miles) of continuous welded rails are now in use.

Published statistics on Chinese railways tend to highlight the growth and developments since 1949 when modern Chinese history began. The following round figures from *China Facts and Figures Annual* Vol 6 1983 are dated to the end of 1981:

| | | |
|---|---|---|
| Length of route | about 50 000 km | about 31 000 miles |
| Railways converted to double track | about 8 000 km | about 5 000 miles |
| Railways electrified | 1 600 km | 1 000 miles |

An illustration of the type of engineering throughout the Chengtu–Kunming Railway, China, opened in July 1970. (Chinese People's Republic Railways)

A 'QJ' class 2–10–2 under construction in Datong Works, about 275 km (170 miles) west of Peking (Beijing), China, on 9 June 1981; the day was the 200th anniversary of the birth of George Stephenson. (John Marshall)

Newly completed 'QJ' class 2–10–2 No 3587 outside Datong Works, China, 9 June 1981. (John Marshall)

Chinese 'SL6' class 4–6–2 No 518 at Juchou on a Shanghai–Canton train, 24 June 1981. (John Marshall)

| | | |
|---|---|---|
| Tunnels built since 1949 | 4 000 | 1 120 miles |
| Total length of these tunnels | 1 800 km | |
| Railway bridges built since 1949 | 14 000 | |
| Total length of these bridges | 1 000 km | 620 miles |
| Tickets sold: 1950 157 500 000 | | |
| 1981 945 000 000 | | |
| Freight hauled (million tonnes): 1950 99.8 | | |
| 1981 1 048 | | |

About 25 per cent of railway hauls are under 100 km. In China the railways carry 70 per cent of the total traffic; river and coastal navigation 13 per cent; highway and air transport 17 per cent.

Steam locomotives still constitute the major source of motive power in China, 77 per cent. In 1980 main-line locomotives were manufactured in six main plants:

Steam locomotives at Datong in Shanxi Province;

Electric locomotives at Zhuzhou in Hunan Province;

Diesel locomotives in four other plants.

Altogether there are 33 plants engaged in making locomotives, rolling stock, parts and equipment. In 1980 they produced 512 locomotives comprising 342 steam, 130 diesel and 40 electric; 1002 passenger cars, and 10 571 freight cars.

# 11 Japanese National Railways

The first railway in Japan, from Yokohama to Sinagawa, was opened on 12 June 1872. It was completed to Tokyo on 14 October. The gauge was 1067 mm (3 ft 6 in) which became the standard gauge in Japan, as in South Africa, New Zealand and parts of Australia. For the Shinkansen (high-speed intercity electric) system, of which the first section opened in 1964, the JNR adopted the general standard gauge, 1435 mm (4 ft 8½ in).

**Railway Development in Japan**

| Year | km | miles | Year | km | miles |
|------|------|------|------|--------|--------|
| 1880 | 158 | 98 | 1940 | 18 399 | 11 433 |
| 1890 | 2 348 | 1 459 | 1950 | 19 786 | 12 295 |
| 1900 | 6 300 | 3 915 | 1960 | 20 403 | 12 678 |
| 1910 | 7 837 | 4 870 | 1970 | 20 814 | 12 933 |
| 1920 | 10 436 | 6 485 | 1980 | 21 322 | 13 248 |
| 1930 | 14 575 | 9 057 | 1981 | 21 419 | 13 309 |

| | km | miles |
|------|------|------|
| Total route length, 1067 mm, 1981 | 21 419 | 13 309 |
| Double and multi-track sections | 5 654 | 3 513 |
| Electrified sections: 1500 V dc | 4 965 | 3 085 |
| 20 kV 60 Hz | 1 458 | 906 |
| 20 kV 50 Hz | 2 012 | 1 250 |
| Total (39.4 per cent of route) | 8 435 | 5 241 |
| Shinkansen, 1435 mm gauge, 25 kV 60 Hz | 1 069 | 664 |
| Length of bridges | 2 362 | 1 468 |

| | km | miles |
|---|---|---|
| Length of tunnels | 1 891 | 1 175 |
| Number of stations | 5 305 | |
| Stations handling passengers and freight | 1 036 | |
| passengers only | 4 149 | |
| freight only | 111 | |
| Train-km, 1981  650 603 000 | | |

| | 1965 | 1975 | 1981 |
|---|---|---|---|
| Passengers carried, millions | 6 722 | 7 048 | 6 793 |
| Passenger-km, millions | 174 014 | 215 289 | 192 115 |
| Freight, millions of tons carried | 200 | 142 | 111 |
| Freight, millions of ton-km | 56 400 | 46 600 | 33 400 |

## Freight Commodities

| Thousands of tons | 1975 | 1980 | 1981 |
|---|---|---|---|
| Petroleum products | 15 738 | 16 500 | 15 055 |
| Coal | 6 729 | 5 891 | 5 763 |
| Ores | 6 146 | 3 913 | 3 256 |
| Limestone | 17 359 | 15 343 | 14 598 |
| Cement | 14 246 | 14 986 | 13 823 |
| Pig iron and steel | 4 212 | 2 368 | 1 963 |
| Timber and lumber | 3 033 | 1 598 | 1 103 |
| Paper and pulp | 5 815 | 3 891 | 3 566 |
| Motor vehicles | 1 050 | 749 | 676 |
| Fertiliser | 6 321 | 5 367 | 4 517 |
| Chemicals | 5 740 | 3 655 | 3 430 |
| Rice | 3 719 | 2 999 | 2 770 |
| Animal feed | 3 559 | 2 873 | 2 275 |
| Fresh fruit and vegetables | 997 | 322 | 240 |
| Fresh and frozen fish | 484 | 196 | 174 |
| Other commodities | 25 130 | 29 026 | 26 390 |

## JAPANESE NATIONAL RAILWAYS

### Freight Vehicles

| | | | |
|---|---|---|---|
| Box cars | 60 134 | Flat cars | 1 619 |
| Refrigerator cars | 1 614 | Container cars | 6 626 |
| Ventilated cars | 74 | Hopper cars | 4 942 |
| Tank cars | 16 | Others | 3 941 |
| Open wagons (gondola cars) | 19 035 | TOTAL | 98 001 |

### Locomotives and Rolling Stock

| | 1975 | 1977 | 1978 | 1979 | 1980 | 1981 |
|---|---|---|---|---|---|---|
| Electric locomotives | 2 051 | 2 049 | 1 978 | 1 936 | 1 856 | 1 760 |
| Diesel locomotives | 2 204 | 2 207 | 2 160 | 2 125 | 2 109 | 2 075 |
| Steam locomotives[1] | 15 | 15 | 5 | 5 | 5 | 5 |
| Electric railcars | 16 502 | 16 843 | 17 247 | 17 462 | 17 696 | 18 144 |
| Diesel railcars | 5 326 | 5 310 | 5 233 | 5 225 | 5 038 | 4 948 |
| Passenger coaches | 6 725 | 6 751 | 6 567 | 6 532 | 6 176 | 6 070 |
| Freight vehicles[2] | 120 597 | 109 890 | 101 042 | 99 846 | 99 562 | 98 001 |

[1] Steam locomotives, except for special trains, were withdrawn in March 1976.
[2] JNR only. Not including privately owned.

| Electric Railcars | 1975 | 1977 | 1978 | 1979 | 1980 | 1981 |
|---|---|---|---|---|---|---|
| Shinkansen traffic | 2 245 | 2 354 | 2 358 | 2 372 | 2 415 | 2 646 |
| Limited express traffic | 2 240 | 2 297 | 2 602 | 2 635 | 2 735 | 2 899 |
| Express and suburban | 6 462 | 6 599 | 6 724 | 6 935 | 6 890 | 7 213 |
| Commuter traffic | 5 298 | 5 325 | 5 293 | 5 276 | 5 383 | 5 214 |

### JNR Container Traffic

| Year | Tons carried, thousands | Ton-km millions |
|---|---|---|
| 1965 | 1 906 | 1 197 |
| 1971 | 10 292 | 7 626 |
| 1972 | 12 394 | 9 419 |

| Year | Tons carried, thousands | Ton-km millions |
|---|---|---|
| 1973 (maximum) | 13 843 | 10 422 |
| 1974 | 12 812 | 9 754 |
| 1975 | 12 114 | 9 378 |
| 1976 | 11 532 | 9 022 |
| 1977 | 10 017 | 8 035 |
| 1978 | 10 286 | 8 387 |
| 1979 | 11 487 | 9 325 |
| 1980 | 9 955 | 8 197 |
| 1981 | 9 244 | 7 788 |

## Number of Trains and Train-km per day, April 1982

| 1067 mm gauge lines | No of trains | Train-km (thousands) |
|---|---|---|
| Passenger trains | 20 703 | 1 218 |
|    Limited express | 650 | 208 |
|    Ordinary express | 817 | 162 |
|    Local | 16 886 | 815 |
|    Deadhead[2] | 2 350 | 33 |
| Express and baggage trains | 143 | 41 |
| Mixed trains | 31 | 2 |
| Freight trains | 3 721 | 366 |
|    Limited express | 80 | 65 |
|    Ordinary express | 65 | 33 |
|    Local | 3 576 | 268 |
| Other trains[1] | 2 349 | 5 |
| Total trains | 26 947 | 1 632 |
| Shinkansen: | | |
| Hikari | 138 | 99 |
| Kodama | 117 | 47 |
| Deadhead[2] | 277 | 6 |
| Total Shinkansen | 532 | 152 |
| Total trains | 27 479 | 1 784 |

[1] Includes service trains and light engines.

[2] Empty stock and non revenue passengers.

|               | 1981    | 1975    |
|---------------|---------|---------|
| Staff employed | 401 362 | 430 051 |

## SHINKANSEN SYSTEM

### Routes

*Tokaido Shinkansen*
  Tokyo–Shin Osaka, 515 km (320 miles)
  Construction period 5½ years. Opened 1 October 1964
  Tunnels 69 km (43 miles), 13 per cent
  Bridges 57 km (35 miles), 11 per cent
  Journey time 3 h 10 min

*Sanyo Shinkansen*
  Shin Osaka–Okayama 161 km (100 miles)
  Construction period 5 years. Opened 15 March 1972
  Tunnels 58 km (36 miles), 36 per cent
  Bridges 20 km (12 miles), 12 per cent
  Journey time 58 min

  Okayama–Hakata 393 km (244 miles)
  Construction period 5 years. Opened 10 March 1975
  Tunnels 223 km (139 miles), 57 per cent
  Bridges 31 km (19 miles), 8 per cent
  Journey time 2 h 28 min

*Tohoku Shinkansen*
  Omiya (Tokyo)–Morioka 465.2 km (290 miles)
  Construction period 10½ years. Opened 23 June 1982
  Tunnels 115 km (71 miles), 23 per cent
  Bridges 78 km (48 miles), 16 per cent
  Journey time 3 h 17 min

*Joetsu Shinkansen*
  Omiya (Tokyo)–Niigata 269.5 km (167 miles)
  Construction period 11 years. Opened 15 November 1982
  Tunnels 106 km (66 miles), 39 per cent
  Bridges 30 km (19 miles), 11 per cent
  Journey time 1 h 45 min

*Shinkansen; general details:*

Track gauge: 1435 mm (4 ft 8½ in)

Rail: 1500 mm (4921 ft) lengths, 60.8 kg/m (137 lb/yd)

Construction gauge: height 7700 mm (25 ft 3 in); width 4400 mm (14 ft 5 in)

Rolling stock: height 5450 mm (17 ft 9 in); width 3400 mm (11 ft 2 in)

Maximum gradients: Tokaido section 20/1000, 1 in 50

Remainder 15/1000, 1 in 66

Minimum curve radius: Tokaido section 2500 mm (8202 ft)

Remainder 4000 m (13 123 ft)

Power system: Tokaido, Sanyo sections 25 kV 60 Hz

Tohoku, Joetsu sections 25 kV 50 Hz

Maximum speed: 210 km/h (130 mph)

## Seikan Tunnel

To link the islands of Honshu and Hokkaido the Seikan Tunnel is being driven beneath the Tsugaru Straits. The tunnel passes through badly fissured rock 100 m (328 ft) below the sea bed which is 140 m (459 ft) deep, a total depth below sea level of 240 m (787 ft). The tunnel will be 53.860 km (33 miles 810 yd) long with 23.3 km (14.4 miles) under the sea. Construction began in 1964 and on 27 January 1983 the pilot bore was holed through. By then 94 per cent of the main tunnel was finished, with less than 3000 m to bore, and it was expected to be completed during 1986. The tunnel will form part of the Shinkansen system.

# 12 Principal Rapid Transit Railways

| Town | First section opened | Gauge, mm | Electrification voltage dc |
|------|------|------|------|
| Amsterdam | 1977 | 1435 | 750 |
| Atlanta, Georgia | 1978 | 1435 | 750 |
| Baku, USSR | 1967 | 1524 | 825 |
| Baltimore | 1983 | 1435 | 650 |
| Barcelona | Dec 1924 | 1674 | 1500 |
| | | 1435 | 1200 |
| Berlin | 1902 | 1435 | 800 |
| Boston, Massachusetts | 1962 | 1435 | 600 |
| Brussels | 20 Sep 1976 | 1435 | 900 |
| Budapest | 1896 | 1435 | 550 |
| Buenos Aires | Dec 1913 | 1435 | A 1100 |
| | | | B 600 |
| | | | C, D, E 1600 |
| Calgary, Alberta | 1981 | 1435 | 600 |
| Chicago, Illinois | 1892 | 1435 | 600 |
| Cleveland, Ohio: | | | |
|   Shaker Heights | 1920 | 1435 | 600 |
|   Rapid Transit | 1955 | 1435 | 600 |
| Edmonton, Alberta | 1978 | 1435 | 600 |
| Frankfurt | 4 Oct 1968 | 1435 | 600 |
| Fukuoka, Japan | 1978 | 1435 | 1500 |
| Glasgow | 14 Dec 1896 | 1219 | 600 |
| Hamburg | 1912 | 1435 | 750 |
| Hanover | 1976 | 1435 | 600 |
| Helsinki | 1982 | 1524 | 750 |
| Hong Kong | 1 Oct 1979 | 1435 | 1500 |

| Town | First section opened | Gauge, mm | Electrification voltage dc |
|---|---|---|---|
| Kharkov | 1974 | 1524 | 825 |
| Kiev, USSR | 1960 | 1520 | 825 |
| Kobe, Japan | Mar 1977 | 1435 | 1500 |
| Leningrad | 1955 | 1524 | 825 |
| Lisbon | 1959 | 1435 | 750 |
| Liverpool (Merseyrail) | 1886 | 1435 | 630 |
| London | 1863 | 1435 | 600 |
| Madrid | 1919 | 1435 | 600 |
| Marseilles | 1978 | 1435 | 750 |
| Mexico City | 1969 | 1435 | 750 |
| Milan, Line 1 | 1 Nov 1964 | 1435 | 750 |
| Line 2 | 4 Oct 1969 | 1435 | 1500 |
| Montreal | 1966 | 1435 | 750 |
| Moscow | 1935 | 1520/24 | 825 |
| Munich | 19 Oct 1971 | 1432 | 750 |
| Nagoya, Japan | 1957 | 1435 | 650 |
| Newcastle upon Tyne | 1980 | 1435 | 1500 |
| New York | 1904 | 1435 | 625 |
| Nuremberg | 1972 | 1435 | 750 |
| Osaka, Japan | 1905 | 1435 | 1500 |
| Oslo | 1966 | 1435 | 750 |
| Paris | 1900 | 1440 | 750 |
| Peking | 1980 | 1435 | 800 |
| Philadelphia, | 1908 | 1581 | 625 |
| Pennsylvania | 1928 | 1435 | 625 |
| Prague | May 1974 | 1435 | 750 |
| Rio de Janeiro | 1982 | 1600 | 750 |
| Rome North | 1932 | 1435 | 3200 |
| South | 1916 | 1435 | 1650 |
| Metropolitan | | | |
| Underground | 10 Feb 1955 | 1435 | 1500 |
| Rome–Ostia–Lido | 1924 | 1435 | 1500 |
| Rotterdam | 9 Feb 1968 | 1435 | 750 |
| San Francisco | 1972 | 1676 | 1000 |
| Santiago, Chile | 1975 | 1676 | 750 |
| São Paulo, Brazil | 26 Sep 1975 | 1600 | 750 |

Tyne & Wear Metro train at Tynemouth, 4 April 1981. (John Marshall)

Slobodskoya Station, Moscow Underground Railway, 27 May 1981. All the stations are richly decorated with mosaics and carvings, and every station is different. (John Marshall)

| Town | First section opened | Gauge, mm | Electrification voltage dc |
|---|---|---|---|
| Sapporo, Japan | 16 Dec 1971 | Rubber tyres in concrete guideway | 750 |
| Seoul, Korea | 1974 | 1435 | 1500 |
| Stockholm, Underground | | 1435 | 650 |
|   Rosagsbanen | | 891 | 1500 |
|   Lidingöbanan | | 1435 | 1500 |
|   Saltsjöbanan | | 1435 | 1500 |
| Stuttgart | 1966 | 1000 | 750 |
| Tashkent, USSR | 1977 | 1520 | 825 |
| Tbilisi, USSR | 1966 | 1524 | 825 |
| Tokyo, Keisei | 1912 | 1435 | 1500 |
|   Underground | 1927 | 1435 and 1067 | 600 and 1500 |
| Toronto | 1954 | 1498 | 600 |
| Tunis | 1874 | 1440 | 750 |
| Vienna, Local | 1898 | 1435 | 850 |
|     Metropolitan | 1974 | 1435 | 750 |
| Washington | 1976 | 1435 | 750 |
| Wuppertal (Suspended railway) | 1 Mar 1901 | mono-rail | 600 |
| Yokohama | 16 Dec 1972 | 1435 | 750 |

Train leaving Kwun Tong, Kowloon, on the Hong Kong Mass Transit Railway, 28 June 1981. (John Marshall)

# 13 The Development of Railway Motive Power

**1803** First locomotive built by Richard Trevithick (qv) for the 914 mm (3 ft) gauge plateway at Coalbrookdale Ironworks, Shropshire. It had a single horizontal cylinder mounted inside the boiler and had flat-tyred wheels with no flanges. A model of it can be seen at the National Railway Museum, York. There is no evidence that this locomotive actually ran.

**1804** Trevithick's second locomotive tested on 22 February on the Penydarren plateway near Merthyr Tydfil in South Wales.

**1805** A third locomotive to Trevithick's design built at Gateshead, County Durham, weighed over 5 tons when completed and was too heavy for the rails; but it was the first locomotive to have flanged wheels.

**1806** Matthew Murray (qv) at Leeds introduced the short 'D' pattern slide valve. He had already built, in 1802, a two-cylinder stationary steam engine with cranks at right angles.

**1811** On 10 April John Blenkinsop (qv) obtained a patent for a steam locomotive propelled by a toothed wheel engaging in a rack on one of the rails.

**1812** A locomotive according to this patent by Matthew Murray went into service on the Middleton Railway, Leeds, on 12 August. It weighed about 5 tons. It was the first commercially successful locomotive. Three more followed and they worked for over 20 years. Similar locomotives were built by Robert Daglish (1777–1865) at Orrell colliery near Wigan in 1812–13.

Spring-loaded safety valve introduced by James Fenton at Leeds. Fenton (1815–63) became a partner of Murray in 1837, in the world's first locomotive works at Leeds.

William Hedley (qv) carried out experiments with a hand-propelled carriage at Wylam, Northumberland, to prove that a locomotive with smooth wheels had adequate adhesion and that Blenkinsop's rack mechanism was unnecessary.

**1813** William Hedley, assisted by Timothy Hackworth (qv) and Jonathan Forster, built his first locomotive at Wylam. It ran on four flanged wheels, and had a boiler 1219 mm (4 ft) diameter and 3048 mm (10 ft) long. Two vertical cylinders at the rear drove the wheels through levers and connecting rods to a centre jack-shaft geared to the two axles. It became known as the *Grasshopper*.

On 22 May William Brunton (1777–1851) patented a locomotive propelled by two legs at the rear. An example was built at Butterley, Derbyshire, for Newbottle colliery near Newcastle.

**1814** George Stephenson (qv) completed his first locomotive, named Blücher, at Killingworth, near Newcastle-upon-Tyne, on 25 July. The two vertical cylinders, mounted along the centre of the boiler, drove the wheels through counter shafts geared to the two driving axles.

**1815** Stephenson and Ralph Dodds at Killingworth patented a locomotive in which the wheels were driven directly and coupled by rods or chains. An example was built using cranked axles coupled by rods, but these proved too weak and they were replaced by chains.

**1816** Loose eccentric valve gear was introduced by George Stephenson with the assistance of Nicholas Wood (1795–1865) and was used on the 'Rocket' and 'Planet' type engines until 1835.

**1818** Valve gear with single fixed eccentric was introduced by Charles Carmichael. The end of the eccentric rod was fixed to two V-shaped 'gabs' in the form of an X which could be raised to engage the forward valve pin or lowered to engage the backward pin. These pins were at opposite ends of a centrally pivoted lever.

**1825** *Locomotion*, No 1, of the Stockton & Darlington Railway, built by George Stephenson, was the first locomotive to have its wheels coupled by rods.

**1826** Sir Goldsworthy Gurney (1793–1875) introduced the multi-jet blast pipe (which had to wait more than a century before its application to locomotives); the fusible plug (a soft metal plug in the firebox crown which melts if uncovered by water and allows steam to damp down the fire); and expansion valve gear (allowing steam to be used expansively).

**1827** Hackworth (qv) built the first six-coupled locomotive, later named *Royal George*, at Shildon, Co Durham. It was also the first locomotive with wheels driven directly from the cylinders.

Multi-tubular boiler patented by Marc Seguin (qv). It was used on a locomotive built by him and first tested on 7 November 1829.

**1828** Stephenson 0–4–0 supplied to the Bolton & Leigh Railway in Lancashire, and named *Lancashire Witch*. It was the first locomotive with its wheels driven directly from the piston rod working in a crosshead.

**1829** The 0–2–2 *Rocket*, mainly designed by Robert Stephenson, won the prize at the Rainhill Trials on the Liverpool & Manchester Railway. It incorporated the direct drive of the *Lancashire Witch*, and also combined a multi-tubular boiler and blast pipe.

Another contestant at Rainhill was *Novelty* by Braithwaite and Ericsson. This was the first inside-cylinder, or inside-connected, locomotive, driven by a crank shaft.

**1830** Stephenson's *Phoenix* for the Liverpool & Manchester Railway was the first locomotive to be built with a smokebox.

Edward Bury (qv) introduced the bar frame and haycock firebox in his 0–4–0 *Liverpool*. It was also one of the first engines to have inside cylinders beneath the smokebox driving onto a cranked axle, which became standard British practice. The bar frame became standard North American practice, following the sale of *Liverpool* to the Petersburg Railroad in 1833.

Stephenson's 2–2–0 *Planet* for the Liverpool & Manchester Railway also incorporated inside cylinders beneath the smokebox and it was the first engine to be built with outside 'sandwich' frames (a slab of oak between iron plates) and outside bearings.

**1831** The 2–2–0 *Union* built by Rothwell Hick & Rothwell of Bolton was the first locomotive to have outside cylinders attached directly to the frame.

**1832** Robert Stephenson experimented with piston valves on a locomotive for the Liverpool & Manchester Railway. He also introduced the 'petticoat blast pipe', by flaring the base of the chimney and extending it downwards to achieve a better smokebox vacuum.

The world's first articulated locomotive, designed by Horatio Allen (qv), built at West Point Foundry, New York, for the South Carolina RR.

**1833** Robert Stephenson's *Patentee* 2–2–2, evolved from *Planet* by adding another pair of wheels behind the firebox, became the first of the 'classic' British single-wheelers. It was the first locomotive to incorporate the steam brake.

The British inside-cylinder 0–6–0 was a straightforward development of the 'Patentee' type in the same year. Another development was the 0–4–2.

On the Dundee & Newtyle Railway, J. & C. Carmichael's 0–2–4 was the first British locomotive to have a bogie.

**1834** Cylindrical smokebox introduced in USA; it became common there by the mid-1850s. In Great Britain it became established about 1900, but the old 'D' pattern was still being made by the LMS and SR in the 1930s and on pannier tanks at Swindon in the 1950s.

Balanced slide valve patented by Hiram Strait in New York. First used on a loco by John Gray (qv) on the Liverpool & Manchester Railway in 1838. An improved pattern was patented in the USA by George W. Richardson in 1872.

**1834–6** 'Gab motion' (valve gear), operated by four fixed eccentrics, first used by Forrester & Co of Liverpool, and by R. & W. Hawthorn of Newcastle-upon-Tyne in 1835. Robert Stephenson & Co used it on the 0–4–2 *Harvey Combe* in 1835.

**1836** Sandboxes first fitted to locomotives in Pennsylvania, USA.

**1837** First American 4–4–0, built in Philadelphia. It had inside cylinders.

**1839** Expansion valve gear first applied to a locomotive by John Gray (qv) on the North Midland Railway. The purpose of the 'horse-leg' motion, as it was known, was to cut off the steam at different positions of the piston stroke to allow the remaining work to be done by the expansion of the steam.

The superheater was introduced on a locomotive by R. & W. Hawthorn of Newcastle-upon-Tyne.

First 'classic' American 4–4–0 produced by Norris of Philadelphia.

**1840** Long-travel valves, giving greater cylinder efficiency, introduced by John Gray on the Hull & Selby Railway.

**1841** First experiments with Hall's brick arch in a locomotive firebox, for smokeless combustion of coal. Several years passed before it came into general use, but it is stated to have been used on the Scottish North Eastern Railway by Thomas Yarrow from about 1857.

First 0–8–0 built by Ross Winans of Baltimore, Maryland, USA.

Sanding gear first applied to a British locomotive by Robert Stephenson.

**1843** Link motion, invented by Howe (qv), but known as 'Stephenson's Link Motion', first used on locomotives built by Robert Stephenson & Co for the North Midland Railway.

'Stationary Link Motion' first used by Daniel Gooch (qv) on the GWR and by his brother John Viret (1812–1900) on the London & South Western Railway.

**1844** Walschaert's valve gear invented by Egide Walschaert (qv) in Belgium. Pneumatic brake invented by James Nasmyth (1808–90), famous for his invention of the steam hammer in 1839.

**1845** Dial pressure gauge, replacing the mercurial gauge, first proposed in Germany by Schinz. It was perfected in 1849 by Eugène Bourdon (1808–84) of Paris.

Balancing of locomotive driving wheels first applied on the London & Birmingham Railway.

**1846** First three-cylinder locomotive built by Robert Stephenson & Co for the Newcastle & Berwick Railway.

First 4–6–0 built by Norris Bros of Philadelphia and delivered to the Philadelphia & Reading RR in 1847.

**1848** Steam brake first used on a locomotive in the USA by George S. Griggs (1805–70) of the Boston & Providence RR.

**1849** Variable cut-off valve gear introduced in the USA by Eltham Rogers, Cleveland, Ohio. First used on a locomotive named *Cleveland* for the Cleveland, Columbus & Cincinnati RR in 1850.

**1850** Compounding of cylinders (in which the steam was used twice, first at boiler pressure and then in partly expanded form at a lower pressure) first tried on the Eastern Counties Railway, England, by its engineer James Samuel (1824–74) who patented it, though it had been invented by John Nicholson in the locomotive department of the railway.

The double-beat regulator valve was introduced by John Ramsbottom (qv) on the LNWR.

First 2–6–0 locomotive built by James Millholland (1812–75) for the Philadelphia & Reading RR.

**1851** Steel tyres for locomotive wheels first produced by Alfred Krupp (1812–87) of Essen, Germany, displayed at the Great Exhibition in London. They were first manufactured by James Millholland of the Philadelphia & Reading RR. Steel tyres lasted for 322 000 to 483 000 km (200 000 to 300 000 miles), compared with 96 500 km (60 000 miles) for iron tyres.

0–4–4–0 articulated locomotive built by John Cockerill & Cie, Belgium, for the Semmering locomotive trials in Austria.

**1852** Edward Bury (qv) introduced the drop grate to facilitate fire cleaning.

J. E. McConnell (1815–83) introduced a smokebox superheater at Wolverton on the LNWR.

**1854** J. H. Beattie (qv) tried out a feed-water heater on the LSWR, first applying it in 1855.

Straight-link motion (valve gear) invented by Alexander Allan (1809–91) and first used on locomotives on the Scottish Central Railway.

**1856** John Ramsbottom (qv) on the LNWR introduced his duplex safety valve, the screw reverser and the displacement lubricator.

**1858** Firehole door deflector plate, assisting combustion, first applied by G. K. Douglas on the Birkenhead, Lancashire & Cheshire Junction Railway.

**1859** Combination of Brick arch and firehole deflector plate, devised by Charles Markham (1823–88), first used on a Midland Railway engine. Markham was assistant to Matthew Kirtley, locomotive superintendent of the MR at Derby.

Steel tyres for locomotives first used on the LNWR.

Steam injector, for forcing water into the boiler against pressure, invented by H. Giffard (qv), first used on locomotives by Sharp Stewart & Co of Manchester.

**1860** Steam injector introduced in the USA by William Sellers (1824–1905).

Steel locomotive firebox first tried on the Scottish Central Railway by Alexander Allan. This became generally used in the USA, but British and European engineers mostly continued with copper fireboxes.

First British 4–4–0 design, by William Bouch (1813–76) appeared on the Stockton & Darlington Railway.

Steel boiler introduced in Canada on 0–6–0 *Scotia* built at Hamilton Works, the first in North America. Before this, boilers were made of wrought iron.

**1862** Steel boilers introduced in Britain by George Tosh on the Maryport & Carlisle Railway.

**1863** Radial axlebox, invented by W. B. Adams (qv), first used on some 2–4–2 tanks built by Cross & Co for the St Helens Railway, Lancashire.

**1864** Belpaire square-shaped firebox, designed by Alfred Belpaire (1820–93) (qv) in Belgium, first used on Belgian State Railways.

Double-bogie articulated locomotive patented by Robert Fairlie (1831–85).

**1865** First 2–8–0, named *Consolidation*, designed by Alexander Mitchell (1832–1908), built by Baldwin Locomotive Works, Philadelphia, USA.

Bristol & Exeter Railway 4–2–4 tank built at Bristol in 1873 as No 39.
Renumbered 2002 on absorption by the Great Western Railway in 1876. It was
converted to a tender engine in 1877 and withdrawn in 1890. The driving wheels'
were 2692 mm (8 ft 10 in). (British Railways)

**1866** 'Pop' safety valves patented by George W. Richardson of the Troy &
Boston RR, USA.

**1867** The 2–10–0 type introduced on the Lehigh Valley RR, USA.

**1871** Inside-cylinder 4–4–0 introduced in Britain by Thomas Wheatley
(1821–83) on the North British Railway.

Compressed-air brake first used on the Caledonian Railway by Steel &
McInnes.

**1874** Non-automatic vacuum brake introduced by J. Y. Smith on the North
Eastern Railway, England.

Pop safety valve, patented in Britain by T. Adams in 1873, first used on a
British locomotive.

Speed indicator used on the London, Brighton & South Coast Railway by
William Stroudley (1833–89).

Steam reversing gear first used by James Stirling (1800–76) on the
Glasgow & South Western Railway.

Patrick Stirling's famous 8 ft single wheeler No 1 of 1870 in steam on the Great Central Railway at Loughborough, Leicestershire, in May 1982. (John Marshall)

The first Garratt locomotive, built by Beyer Peacock & Co, Manchester, England, in 1909, for the 762 mm (2 ft 6 in) gauge North East Dundas Tramway, Tasmania. National Railway Museum, York, 15 February 1979. (John Marshall)

Walschaert's valve gear first used in the USA by William Mason (1808–83) on the Boston, Clinton & Fitchburg RR.

**1876** Hydraulic brake introduced by Francis William Webb (1836–1906) on the LNWR.

First compound locomotive, by A. Mallet (qv), in France.

Davies & Metcalfe exhaust-steam injector, making use of exhaust steam to force water into the boiler against full steam pressure.

**1877** Wide firebox invented by John E. Wootten (1822–98) when general manager of the Philadelphia & Reading RR. It was intended for burning anthracite waste, or culm. First used on a P & R 4–6–0 No 411 in 1880.

**1878** Automatic vacuum brake, invented by James Gresham (1836–1914).

First 2–6–0s in Britain, designed by William Adams (1823–1904) on the Great Eastern Railway.

**1879** Joy's radial valve gear, invented by David Joy (qv), tried on a Bury 0–4–0 on the Furness Railway, England. It took its drive off the connecting rod, so dispensing with eccentrics.

**1883–4** First regular use of oil fuel on locomotives, on the Russian South Eastern Railway, using the Urquhart system.

**1884** Mallet type articulated locomotive patented by Anatole Mallet (qv).

**1886** Steel plate frames introduced by Webb on the LNWR at Crewe.

East African Railways metre-gauge Class EC3 4–8–2 + 2–8–4 Garratt No 5903 built by Beyer Peacock, Manchester (No 7634) in 1955. Coupled wheels 1372 mm (4 ft 6 in). Weight 251.68 tons. Latterly the EC3s were the largest steam locomotives at work in the world. (Greater Manchester Museum of Science and Industry)

First British 0–8–0s, on the Barry Railway in South Wales.

Steam sanding gear, devised by James Gresham (see above) and Francis Holt (1825–93, works manager, Midland Railway, Derby) introduced on the MR. It brought about a revival of the 'single-wheeler' locomotive, and the famous series of MR 4–2–2s.

First 4–6–2 type locomotive built by Vulcan Iron Works, Pennsylvania, to a design by G. S. Strong, for the Lehigh Valley RR.

**1887** Oil fuel first used on locomotives in Britain (GER) and in the USA (Pennsylvania RR).

**1888** First 4–4–2 type locomotive, also designed by Strong for the Lehigh Valley RR, built by Vulcan Iron Works. The type name 'Atlantic' appeared in 1894.

**1892** First British inside-cylinder 0–8–0 built at Crewe to a design by F. W. Webb.

**1894** First 4–6–0 to run in Britain introduced on the Highland Railway by David Jones (1834–1906).

**1895** American type long smokebox appeared on the GWR in England. Extended smokeboxes had been tried by Hugh Smellie on the Glasgow & South Western Railway in 1886, and on the Great Eastern and Mersey Railways.

**1897** Four-cylinder simple-expansion locomotive introduced in Britain by James Manson (1846–1935) on the Glasgow & South Western Railway, on 4–4–0 No 11.

Smoke-tube superheater introduced in Germany by Wilhelm Schmidt (qv).

The first of the British Railways standard steam locomotives, designed under the supervision of R. A. Riddles, 4–6–2 No 70 000 *Britannia*, on 17 June 1978, shortly after completion of rebuilding at Bridgnorth on the Severn Valley Railway. (John Marshall)

The last steam locomotive built by British Railways, completed at Swindon in March 1959, standard 2–10–0 No 92220 *Evening Star*, at Bewdly on the Severn Valley Railway, on 18 May 1983. (John Marshall)

British Railways Class 4 4–6–0 No 75069 being shunted at Bewdley on the Severn Valley Railway on 6 July 1974, shortly after it had been acquired from a scrap yard. (John Marshall)

The same locomotive as in the previous photograph, entering Bewdley on 27 August 1984, soon after returning to traffic following complete rebuilding at Bridgnorth, mostly by voluntary labour. (John Marshall)

First 2−8−2 locomotives built by Baldwin Locomotive Works for Japanese Railways. From these arose the type name 'Mikado'.

**1898** First British 'Atlantic' type locomotive, GNR No 990, by H. A. Ivatt (qv).

First diesel engine demonstrated by Dr Rudolph Diesel (1858−1913).

**1899** First British 4−6−0 passenger engine built by the NER to a design by Wilson Worsdell (1850−1920).

Smokebox superheater applied to 4−4−2 No 737 by J. A. F. Aspinall (qv) on the Lancashire & Yorkshire Railway. This was the first British superheated locomotive.

**1900** First 2−6−2 tender engine built by Baldwin Locomotive Works for the Chicago, Burlington & Quincy RR. Use on mid-west lines gave origin to the type name 'Prairie'.

**1901** First use of a superheater in North America, on Canadian Pacific 4−6−0 No 548.

**1902** The wide firebox introduced on the Great Northern Railway, England, on a 4−4−2 by H. A. Ivatt (qv).

First British 0−10−0, built by James Holden (qv) on the GER.

**1903** 'Santa Fe' 2−10−2 type introduced on the Atcheson, Topeka & Santa Fe RR.

The 2−8−0 type introduced in Britain by Churchward (qv) on the GWR.

**1905** Poppet valve gear first applied to a locomotive in Germany by Hugo Lentz (qv).

Mechanical stokers introduced on Pennsylvania RR 2−8−2s.

**1906** Smoke-tube superheater first used in Britain by Churchward (qv) on GWR 4−6−0 No 2901 and by George Hughes (1860−1945) on two Lancashire & Yorkshire Railway 0−6−0s.

**1907** 'Garratt' articulated locomotive patented by Herbert William Garratt (qv).

**1908** First British 4−6−2 'Pacific' locomotive, No 111 *The Great Bear*, built at Swindon by the GWR under Churchward.

First steam turbine locomotive, 0−4−0 tank designed by Prof Belluzzo, built in Milan by S. A. Officine Mechaniche.

**1910** Steam-turbine-electric locomotive designed by Sir Hugh Reid and

W. M. Ramsey and built by the North British Locomotive Co, Glasgow, of which Reid (1860–1935) was chairman and chief managing director.

**1912–13** First diesel locomotive, an experimental 1000 hp direct-drive Diesel-Klose-Sulzer unit, built by the North British Locomotive Co.

**1913** First diesel railway vehicle in revenue service, Atlas-Deva 75 bhp diesel-electric railcar in Sweden. It ran until 1939.

**1920** Caprotti valve gear first used, on a 2–6–0 in Italy. (See Caprotti, p. 25.)

**1922** First British 'production' 4–6–2s built by the GNR.

**1923** First commercially successful diesel-electric locomotive in the USA, a 300 hp unit by the American Locomotive Co (ALCO), with Ingersoll-Rand engine and General Electric Co controls and transmission.

**1924** First experiments with diesel traction in Britain, on the LNER.

**1925** First 'main line' diesel electric locomotives, four 1200 hp units built for German State Railways to a design by Prof George V. Lomonosoff (1876–1952).

Cast-steel single-unit engine-bed, or frame, introduced in North America by General Steel Castings Corporation. By 1930 the castings included cylinders, valve chambers and smokebox saddle.

**1928** First British diesel-electric train, converted from a former Lancashire & Yorkshire Railway electric train by fitting it with a 500 hp Beardmore engine.

**1929** Experimental four-cylinder high-pressure compound 4–6–4 No 10 000 with water-tube boiler and pressure of 450 lb/in$^2$ (31.6 kg/cm$^2$), designed by Gresley (qv) and built by the LNER.

Experimental three-cylinder high-pressure compound 4–6–0 No 6399 *Fury* built by the North British Locomotive Co, Glasgow, for the LMS.

**1931** First diesel locomotive in regular service in Britain, rebuilt from a Midland Railway 0–6–0 tank by the LMS. It had a Paxman engine with Haslam & Newton hydrostatic transmission.

**1932** First high-speed diesel train, *The Flying Hamburger*, scheduled to run at 161 km/h (100 mph) between Berlin and Hamburg.

**1933** Stanier 4–6–2 design introduced on the LMS.

**1934** First diesel-electric streamlined train, the *Burlington Zephyr* of the Chicago, Burlington & Quincy Railroad. On 26 May it travelled 1633 km (1015 miles) from Denver to Chicago non stop at an average speed of 125 km/h (77.6 mph).

**1935** Direct-drive turbine 4–6–2 No 6202 designed by Stanier (qv) and built by the LMS.

First British streamlined steam locomotives, Gresley's 'A4' class 4–6–2s, introduced by the LNER.

**1937** Stanier's streamlined 4–6–2 introduced on the LMS.

**1938** First British streamlined diesel train built by the LMS.

**1939** General Motors 'Electro Motive' No 103 built in USA. It was a four-unit freight locomotive of 5400 hp. In a year it covered 133 570 km (83 000 miles) on 21 systems in 37 States in temperatures from −40° to +43.3°C (−40° to +110°F) at altitudes from sea level to 3109 m (10 200 ft). Its performance on long steep grades with heavy trains established the future of the diesel-electric locomotive and the fate of the steam locomotive.

**1941** First gas-turbine-electric locomotive built for Swiss Federal Railways by Brown Boveri & Co of Baden.

**1947** First main-line diesel-electric locomotives on a British railway, built by the LMS.

Danish State Railways (DSB) Co–Co diesel-electric locomotive No 1437 at Copenhagen Central station on 26 April 1979. These 3900 hp machines are the most powerful diesel-electric units in Europe. (John Marshall)

**1948** First gas-turbine-electric locomotives in the USA, built by the General Electric Co for the Union Pacific RR.

**1949** Budd diesel railcars introduced in North America.

**1950** Gas-turbine-electric locomotive introduced in Britain by the Western Region, A1A–A1A No 18000 built by Brown Boveri Co.

**1952** British-built gas-turbine-electric locomotive, No 18100, entered service in January on the Western Region.

**1954** Diesel multiple-unit trains introduced on British Railways.

**1955** First of the 'Deltic' diesels built by the English Electric Co at the Vulcan Works, Lancashire. The 22 production units from 1961 each ran well over 2 million miles at speeds of up to 161 km/h (100 mph).

**1957** Diesel-electric multiple-unit trains introduced on the Southern Region of British Railways.

**1958** First British main-line diesel-hydraulic locomotive, A1A–A1A No D600, built by the North British Locomotive Co for the Western Region of BR. Hydraulic transmission was adopted by the Western Region in preference to electric. It had the advantage of lower weight in relation to power output, but maintenance costs were said to be high. Altogether the Western Region had 309 diesel-hydraulic main-line locomotives in six classes. The last were withdrawn in 1977, but several have been preserved.

**1969** The world's largest and most powerful single-unit diesel-electric locomotive, the Do-Do 'Centennial' class of 6600 hp, was introduced by the Union Pacific RR, USA.

**1972** Prototype gas-turbine-driven TGV (Train à Grande Vitesse) tested on French Railways. (For details of electric TGVs see p 79.)

## LOCOMOTIVE CLASSIFICATION

Steam locomotive types were originally described by various cumbrous methods, such as 'four-wheels coupled locomotive with leading bogie and two-wheeled trailing truck'. The system of 'wheel arrangements' was invented in 1900 by an American locomotive engineer, Frederic M. Whyte (1865–1941). By this system, the above locomotive is simply a 4–4–2. Despite the obvious advantage and simplicity of the Whyte system, many locomotive engineers continued to use the old cumbrous system well into the twentieth century. Driving or coupled wheels are always in the centre;

leading or trailing wheels are denoted by 0, 2, 4 or 6. In the following examples the locomotives are imagined facing to the left:

| | |
|---|---|
| ○○OO | 4–4–0 |
| ○O○ | 2–2–2 |
| ○OOO○ | 2–6–2 |
| OO○○ | 0–4–4 |
| OOO | 0–6–0 |
| ○OOOO | 2–8–0 |
| ○OOOOO○○ | 2–10–4 |
| ○○OOO OOO○○ | 4–6–6–4 (Mallet articulated type) |

Tank locomotives are generally denoted by a letter T, eg: 0–6–2T; a saddle tank by ST, eg: 0–6–0ST.

The European continental countries use an axle system, thus a 4–6–2 is a 2C1 or, in France, a 2 3 1. Germany and Switzerland denoted the number of driving axles as a fraction of the total number of axles. In this system the 4–6–2 is a 3/6, a 2–8–0 a 4/5, a 0–6–0 a 3/3. It fails to give a precise definition of the type because, for example, a 3/5 could be a 4–6–0, a 2–6–2 or a 0–6–4. Germans refer to a tank locomotive as a 'Tender Lokomotive', ie a locomotive carrying its own tender. A tender locomotive is known as a 'Lokomotive mit Schlepptender', or a 'locomotive with dragged tender'.

Many countries incorporated an axle or classification system with the engine number. The French, for example, numbered an engine 231.D.686 which was 'D' class 4–6–2 No 686. The Germans incorporated a class number, eg 41.255, or Class 41 No 255. British Railways adopted this system in 1968. Diesel classes are numbered 01 to 58 with many gaps where classes have been withdrawn, and electric classes from 70 to 87. For example, diesel-electric locomotive No 50 023 is '50' class No 23.

Classification of electric and diesel locomotives is on a different system, using a letter to denote the number of driving axles: A is one; B is two; C three and D four. A locomotive on two four-wheeled bogies with a motor to each axle is a Bo–Bo. The small 'o' indicates that the axles are not coupled. If the wheels were coupled it would be a BB. A locomotive on two six-wheeled bogies with all axles driven but not coupled is a Co–Co; if the axles are coupled it is a CC: if the centre axle is not driven it is an A1A–A1A. If the trucks are articulated by a connection taking buffing and drag stresses a plus sign is used; for example the locomotives of the Furka-Oberalp and Brig-Visp-Zermatt Railways in Switzerland are Bo + Bo.

# 14 Progress of Railway Electrification

**1831** Michael Faraday (1791–1867) discovered the principle of magnetic induction, leading to the invention of the dynamo.

**1833** Rotative dynamo demonstrated by Joseph Saxton in Cambridge in June. The machine was not perfected until after 1870.

**1835** An experimental electric railway, in model form, was made by Thomas Davenport, a blacksmith in Vermont, USA. The form of the motor is not known. On 25 February 1837 Davenport patented an electric motor.

**1842** Robert Davidson tested a battery-driven electric locomotive weighing 5 tons on the Edinburgh & Glasgow Railway where it ran at 6.5 km/h (4 mph).

**1873** DC commutator motor invented by Zénobe Gramme (1826–1901) of Belgium.

**1879** First practical electric railway built by German engineer Werner von Siemens (qv) for the Berlin Trades Exhibition. It operated from 31 May to 30 September on an oval track about 300 m (328 yd) long with a gauge of 1 m. The locomotive had a 3 hp motor, picking up current at 150 V dc from a centre third rail and returning it via the wheels and running rails. It could pull about 30 passengers on three cars at 6.5 km/h (4 mph).

**1880–4** Thomas Edison (1847–1931) carried out experiments with electric railways at his works Menlo Park in New Jersey.

**1881** First public electric railway in the world opened at Lichtefelde, near Berlin, on 12 May. It was 2.5 km (1½ miles) long. The car ran on a 100 V supply and carried 26 passengers at 48 km/h (30 mph).

**1883** Volk's Electric Railway opened on 4 August at Brighton (see Magnus Volk), with a gauge of 610 mm (2 ft). It was rebuilt to 838 mm (2 ft 9 in) gauge and extended, and re-opened on 4 April 1884.

Portrush–Giant's Causeway Tramway formally opened on 28 September in Ireland. It was the first railway to run on hydro-electric power.

First standard-gauge electric locomotive in the USA built by Leo Daft for the Saratoga & Mount Macgregor Railroad. It was named *Ampère*.

**1888** AC electric motor invented in the USA by Nikola Tesla (1856–1943), a Yugoslav by birth.

**1890** City & South London Railway opened on 18 December, the first electric underground railway, using four-wheeled electric locomotives built by Mather & Platt, Salford, Lancashire. One is preserved in the Science Museum, London.

**1893** First section of the Liverpool Overhead Railway opened on 6 March, the first elevated electric city railway. It was completed to Dingle (underground!) on 21 December 1896. It used a third rail system at 500 V dc.

**1895** First electric train service in the USA started on 28 June on the 11 km (7 mile) Nantasket branch of the New York, New Haven & Hartford Railroad.

Electric locomotives introduced on 4 August on goods trains on the Baltimore & Ohio Railroad, on the Belt line from Henrietta Street, Baltimore (just south of Camden Station), to Waverley Tower, 6 km ($3\frac{3}{4}$ miles) through ten tunnels amounting to 48 per cent of the distance. First trials were on 27 June 1895. Overhead slot pickup was used at first, replaced by a third rail in March 1902.

Electric trains introduced on the Chicago Elevated Railway.

System of multiple-unit control for electric trains without locomotives perfected by Frank Julian Sprague (1857–1934) in the USA. It was first used on the Chicago South Side Elevated Railway in 1897.

**1899** Burgdorf–Thun Railway, Switzerland, began operation on 21 July using a three-phase system at 750 V $16\frac{2}{3}$ Hz on its 40 km (25 miles) of route. This was the first alternating current system.

**1901–3** Tests carried out by Siemens and Allgemeine Elektrizitäts–Gesellschaft, Berlin (AEG) on the Zossen–Marienfeld line near Berlin with two test cars and a test locomotive. The test cars reached a record speed of 217 km/h (135 mph). The system was 10 000 V three-phase 50 Hz overhead, transformed on the vehicle to 1150 V (Siemens) and 435 V (AEG).

**1902** Berlin Elevated Railway began operation, as an electric line from the start.

**1903** Electrification introduced on the Mersey Railway on 3 May, using a third rail at 600 V dc. This was the first British steam railway to be electrified. It now forms part of the modern Merseyrail system.

**1904** Single-phase ac system introduced on the Seebach–Wettingen Railway, Switzerland. At first it had a 50 Hz supply, with dc traction motors supplied by a motor-generator, but before opening it was rebuilt for 15 000 V 15 Hz with ac traction motors. The first single-phase locomotive is preserved in the Swiss Transport Museum, Lucerne. The use of a low frequency was the result of work by Hans Behn-Eschenburg (1864–1938) of Zurich who found that this overcame commutation difficulties. For further electrification in Switzerland the frequency of 16⅔ Hz was adopted, one third of the standard 50 Hz frequency of the commercial supply.

First British suburban railway electrification schemes brought into operation. On 29 March the first of the Tyneside lines of the North Eastern Railway between Newcastle and Benton; and on 5 April the Lancashire & Yorkshire line from Liverpool to Southport. Both used a third rail at 600 V dc.

**1905** Metropolitan–District 'Inner Circle' in London electrified on 12 September with 600 V dc third rail. The last steam trains ran on 23 September.

**1907** Electrification brought into operation on the New York, New Haven & Hartford Railroad to coincide with the electrification of New York Grand Central Station and approaches. The New Haven line used 11 000 V 15 Hz overhead and the terminal lines 600 V dc. Locomotives, built by Baldwin–Westinghouse, were designed to operate right through on both systems.

Misox Railway opened on 6 May between Bellinzona and Mesocco in Ticino, Switzerland. This 32 km (20 mile) metre-gauge line was the first to use a 1500 V dc overhead system which became a world standard.

**1908** The Midland Railway, England, introduced electric trains between Morecambe and Heysham on 1 February, using an experimental 6600 V single-phase ac system at 25 Hz. Electrification was extended to Lancaster Castle station on 14 September. The power cars had ac commutator motors. In 1953 the line was rebuilt with ac at 50 Hz, still at 6600 V, to test this frequency before the decision to adopt 25 kV 50 Hz as the standard. (See 1953 below.)

**1913** First section of the metre-gauge Rhaetian Railway in Switzerland to be electrified began operation on 1 July between St Moritz and Schuls, 62 km (38.5 miles), using 11 000 V 16⅔ Hz. Its success, and that of the 15 000 V 16⅔ Hz on the Lötschberg Railway, also in 1913, influenced the

Car at Children's Playground station, Volks Electric Railway, Brighton. (John Marshall)

One of the earliest single-phase electric locomotives, 1B1 No 207 of 1913, at Samaden on the metre-gauge Rhaetian Railway, Switzerland, on 8 August 1966. (John Marshall)

Trondheim train about to leave Oslo, Norway, on 28 April 1979. Electrification is at 15 kV 16⅔ Hz, as in Austria, Germany and Switzerland. (John Marshall)

A Manchester to Sheffield train at Penistone on 14 May 1966, hauled by 1500 V dc Co–Co locomotive No 27005 *Minerva*. Following withdrawal in 1970, the entire class of seven locomotives was sold to Netherlands Railways. (John Marshall)

The most powerful locomotive type on British Railways: an '87' class Bo–Bo electric locomotive at Preston on the 25 kV London–Glasgow main line. This type hauls trains of 500 tons or more at 161 km/h (100 mph). (John Marshall)

Train on the Black Mesa & Lake Powell Railroad, Arizona, approaching the loading terminal, on 9 October 1983. This, the world's first 50 kV 50 Hz electric railway, 125.5 km (78 miles) long, was opened on 15 March 1974 to carry coal to a power station near Lake Powell. (John Marshall)

adoption of the latter for further electrification in Switzerland and also in Austria, Germany, Norway and Sweden.

Experimental electrification by Dick, Kerr, of Preston, on 29 July on the Bury–Holcombe Brook branch of the Lancashire & Yorkshire Railway, using a 3500 V dc overhead system.

**1915** Electrification on the 29.8 km (18½ mile) Shildon–Newport line of the North Eastern Railway, 1 July, so introducing the 1500 V dc overhead system into Britain. It was proposed to adopt this between York and Newcastle, but shortage of money after World War I prevented further progress.

The 1500 V dc system was recommended for adoption as the British standard for main line electrification by the 1921 'Electrification Committee' Report and by the subsequent Pringle (1928) and Weir (1931) Reports.

**1916** Electric trains introduced on 17 April between Manchester and Bury, on a 1200 V dc third rail system with side contact. This is the highest permitted voltage with a third rail.

**1930** The first mercury-arc rectifier to be installed on a British railway brought into use at Hendon on the Morden–Edgware line of the London Underground. It was an important technical improvement, making unmanned substations possible. Previously, permanently-manned rotary converters had to be used.

**1931** The first British passenger railway to be equipped with a 1500 V dc overhead system, the Manchester South Junction & Altrincham, brought into operation on 8 May with multiple-unit trains.

**1933** First British main-line electrification, on 1 January, from London to Brighton, using 660 V third rail.

Kando system of 50 Hz electrification, first tried in Hungary in 1923, installed on the Budapest–Hegyeshalom line, 191 km (119 miles), using current at 16 000 V converted to three-phase on the Bo–Co locomotives for traction by rotary converters.

**1936** Further experiments with 50 Hz traction on the Höllental (Black Forest) section of German State Railways, at 20 000 V. Four experimental locomotives were built, two with rectifiers and dc motors, one on the Kando system with rotary converter, and the fourth with 50 Hz motors.

**1950–1** As a result of the Höllental line coming into the French zone after World War II, the French Railways decided to install a 50 Hz system, at 25 kV, on the Aix-les-Baines to La Roche-sur-Foron line of the South Eastern Region, 89 km (55 miles). Two locomotives had 50 Hz motors and

179

a third had a rotary converter and dc traction motors.

**1953** British Railways experimented with 50 Hz electrification, at 6600 V, on the former Midland Railway section from Lancaster to Heysham using mercury-arc rectifiers in the power cars and dc traction motors. Services began on 17 August.

**1954** Passenger service inaugurated on 14 September between Manchester and Sheffield on 'Britain's first all-electric main line' (freight and passenger), with the 1500 V dc overhead system.

**1956** Decision made on 6 March to adopt 25 kv 50 Hz as the future British standard. By this time rectifiers were being developed suitable for locomotives and power cars.

**1959** Electrification at 25 kv 50 Hz brought into operation on 16 March on the Colchester—Clacton—Walton line of BR Eastern Region, providing an improved service using multiple-unit trains.

**1960—1** Germanium and silicon rectifiers introduced by BR on ac locomotives and railcars.

**1960** First portion of BR London Midland Region main line electrification at 25 kV opened on 12 September between Crewe and Manchester. Crewe to Liverpool followed on 1 January 1962. Full service to London began on 18 April 1966 and to Glasgow on 6 May 1974.

The 25 kV 50 Hz system is being adopted as a standard for new electrification throughout the world. It was introduced in the following countries: Zaire (formerly Belgian Congo) 1952; Hungary 1954; Turkey, USSR 1955; East Germany, Luxembourg 1956; Portugal 1957; China 1958; Czechoslovakia 1962; Japan 1964; Roumania 1965; Jugoslavia 1968; India 1969; Pakistan 1970.

**1961** Rheostatic braking introduced by BR on ac locomotives. First BR ac locomotive with transductor control relieving contactors of arc rupturing. Delivery took place of the first BR 'electro-diesel' locomotives of Class 73 for use on and off the Southern Region third rail dc system. These BoBo locomotives can work on the third rail at 750 V with an output of 1600 hp or as diesel-electrics of 600 hp.

**1962** The first silicon rectifier locomotive in the USA, one of six, was delivered on 3 July to the Pennsylvania RR as No 4460.

**1974** The world's first 50 kV railway opened on 15 March between Black Mesa mines near Kayenta, Arizona, USA, and the Navajo Power Station, near Lake Powell: the standard-gauge Black Mesa & Lake Powell RR, 125.5 km (78 miles). The high voltage requires only one feed point at one end of the line.

In South Africa a new 1065 mm (3 ft 6 in) gauge line on 50 kV 50 Hz began operation between Sishen and Saldanha Bay, north of Cape Town, 846 km (525 miles), on 7 May 1976.

In Northern Brazil the 1600 mm (5 ft 3 in) gauge single-line Carajás ore railway, 890 km (553 miles) long, was due to open in 1984, using a 50 kV 60 Hz system.

1975 The first BR ac locomotive with thyristor control, No 87 101, built at Crewe. The thyristor gives notchless control at constant tractive effort, while tap-changer control produces variations in tractive effort in each notch.

Chopper circuits, now being used to control some electric locomotives, are solid-state switches capable of rapid closing and opening for controlling the voltage applied to dc traction motors. They consist of thyristors in conjunction with diodes, and capacitors to give continuous current flow. Chopper control results in a 20–25 per cent improvement in energy consumption and also facilitates regenerative braking.

The world's most powerful electric locomotives with chopper control, to be built as a production series, are the 7000 hp CoCo type supplied by ACEC (Ateliers de Constructions Electriques de Charleroi Société Anonyme, part of the Westinghouse Electric Group), and La Brugeoise et Nivelles, for the 3000 V dc Belgian National Railways (SNCB) and first delivered on 9 September 1975. They represented a great advance in the use of semiconductors for traction-power conversion.

## Railway Electrification in Europe

| Country | Route km | Electrified km | Percentage |
|---|---|---|---|
| Austria | 5 854 | 2 850 | 48.7 |
| Belgium | 3 998 | 1 296 | 32.4 |
| Bulgaria | 4 045 | 1 326 | 32.8 |
| Czechoslovakia | 13 241 | 2 684 | 20.2 |
| Denmark | 2 004 | 101 | 5.0 |
| Finland | 6 069 | 516 | 8.5 |
| France | 34 362 | 10 074 | 29.3 |
| Germany DB | 28 450 | 10 602 | 37.3 |
| DR | 14 215 | 1 123 | 7.9 |
| Great Britain | 17 229 | 3 752 | 21.7 |

| Country | Route km | Electrified km | Percentage |
|---|---|---|---|
| Hungary | 7 483 | 1 211 | 16.2 |
| Italy | 16 133 | 8 374 | 51.9 |
| Netherlands | 2 850 | 1 731 | 60.7 |
| Norway | 4 241 | 1 440 | 57.5 |
| Poland | 23 855 | 5 943 | 24.9 |
| Portugal | 2 883 | 458 | 15.9 |
| Roumania | 11 083 | 1 296 | 11.7 |
| Spain | 13 531 | 4 374 | 32.3 |
| Sweden | 11 195 | 6 959 | 62.2 |
| Switzerland (SBB only) | 2 934 | 2 918 | 99.4 |
| Yugoslavia | 9 762 | 2 649 | 27.1 |

West Germany (DB) has the greatest length of electrified route in Europe, 10 602 km (6 589 miles), 37.26 per cent of its total, followed by France with 10 074 km (6260 miles), 29.3 per cent. The system with the highest percentage is the Swiss Federal Railways, 2918 km (1812 miles) electrified out of a total of 2934 km (1823 miles), 99.4 per cent. (See p 181.)

# 15 Railway Tunnels over 5000 m Long

The world's longest railway tunnel forms part of the Moscow underground system. It is Line 6 from Belgaevo to Medvedkovo, about 30.1 km (18.7 miles). This is in tunnel throughout and, including termini, has 19 stations.

Next in length are Line 1 of the Leningrad underground system from Veteranov to Komsomolskaya, about 30 km (18.6 miles) with 19 stations, and Line 3 at Moscow from Kakhovskaya to Rechnoi Vokzal, about 29.3 km (18.2 miles). These are also entirely underground except for Komsomolskaya station.

The world's longest railway tunnel open at both ends is on the London Underground railway system from East Finchley to Morden via Bank, 27.842 km (17 miles 528 yd). There are 25 stations and 3 junctions in the tunnel.

The longest railway tunnel in North America is the Henderson Tunnel in Colorado. It is really a long mine adit about 15.4 km (9.6 miles) long, leading into a molybdenum mine near Empire 64 km (40 miles) west of Denver. The exact length of the tunnel is difficult to establish because one end is inside the mine.

On the Canadian Pacific Railway a new tunnel is being driven under Rogers Pass at a lower level than the Connaught tunnel. It will be 14 723 m (9 miles 260 yd) long.

In Japan the Seikan tunnel under the sea between Honshu and Hokkaido (see p 151) will be 53.850 km (33 miles 810 yd) long when completed. It will be the longest railway tunnel in the world, and the lowest point on any main-line railway.

## Channel Tunnel Chronology

**1874** Powers obtained by the South Eastern Railway of England to sink experimental shafts.

**1881** SER obtained powers to acquire lands between Dover and Folkestone. Submarine Continental Railway Co incorporated on 12 December to take over the SER works. Sir John Hawkshaw (qv) appointed engineer. A pilot tunnel 1920 m (2100 yd) was driven out under the sea.

**1875** A Channel Tunnel Co and a French Submarine Railway Co obtained powers to carry out works. French company drove a 2414 m ($1\frac{1}{2}$ mile) tunnel under the sea from Sangatte.

**1883** Submarine Continental Railway Co suspended work.

**1886** English company absorbed by the Submarine Continental Co.

**1887** Name of company changed to Channel Tunnel Co.

**1923** Original SER interests passed to the Southern Railway on 1 January.

**1948** SR interests passed to British Railways on 1 January.

**1957** Channel Tunnel Study Group formed in July to carry out extensive economic, traffic, revenue and engineering studies.

**1960** Report submitted in March, recommending a twin railway tunnel.

**1964** On 6 February the British and French Governments decided to go ahead with the project.

**1965** Survey work completed in October. The Dover Strait is about 34 km (21 miles) wide with a maximum depth of water of about 61 m (200 ft). The tunnel will pass through the Lower Chalk strata at a depth of about 49 m (160 ft) below the sea bed, with gradients of 1 in 100, or 1 per cent. It will be about 51.5 km (32 miles) long. A pilot tunnel bored ahead of the main tunnel will act as a probe to detect any water ingress.

**1973** Cost of tunnel estimated at £468 million, of which the British and French Channel Tunnel Companies would each contribute half.

**1974** In November the British Government decided to abandon the proposed high-speed rail link to London on grounds of expense.

**1975** In January the British Government decided to abandon its support of the entire Channel Tunnel project, after considerable construction work had already been carried out. This was seen by the French as a disgraceful failure of commitment.

**1977** On 4 July a vote in the European Parliament was in favour of a viability study.

**1978** Discussions between British Railways Board and French Railways on the possibility of making a single-line bore as a first step, using a 'tidal flow' system of operation which could handle an estimated 8 000 000 passengers and 8 000 000 tons of freight a year. Doubling with a second tunnel could follow later.

**1981** An all-party committee of MPs reported on 6 March in favour of a 7 m (23 ft) diameter tunnel. Ferry operators wanted a 6 m (19 ft 8 in) tunnel to prevent lorries being taken through and to force them to use the ferries. The French Government was not forthcoming at this stage in view of the earlier behaviour of the British Government. Two companies, Tarmac and Wimpey, joined forces to promote a plan to finance, build and operate the tunnel.

**1982** On 3 March, at a joint French and British meeting, it was agreed to make a 7 m diameter tunnel with duplication at a later date. The British Government was still obsessed with ideological objections to the provision of financial guarantees, but the French demanded a solid commitment to the project.

**1984** A report drawn up by a group of five French and British banks recommended that a twin railway tunnel, capable of taking all sizes of motor vehicles on special wagons and costing £8 billion, would be economically viable. Robert Reid, chairman of BR, and Charles Fiterman, French Transport Minister, both stressed the urgency of making a decision to proceed. Although the project would not involve tax-payers' money, firm political support from both governments was essential.

Swiss end of the Simplon Tunnel at Brig, 28 July 1966. The first tunnel (left) 19 803 m (12 miles 537 yds) long, was opened on 1 June 1906 and the second, 19 823 m (12 miles 559 yds), on 16 October 1922. (John Marshall)

| Tunnel | m | Date | Railway | Position |
|---|---|---|---|---|
| Seikan | 53 850 | [1] | Japanese National | Honshu–Hokkaido |
| Daishimizu | 22 228 | 3.1980 | Japanese National | Jōmō-Kōgen–Echigo |
| Simplon No 2 | 19 823 | 16.10.1922 | Swiss Federal | Brig–Iselle |
| Simplon No 1 | 19 803 | 1.6.1906 | Swiss Federal | Brig–Iselle |
| Shin Kanmon | 18 713 | 10.3.1975 | Japanese National | Honshu–Kyushu |
| Apennine | 18 519 | 12.4.1934 | Italian State | Florence–Bologna |
| Rokko | 16 250 | 15.3.1972 | Japanese National | Osaka–Shinkobe |
| Furka Base | 15 381 | 28.6.1982 | Furka Oberalp | Oberwald–Realp |
| Haruna | 15 350 | 15.11.1982 | Japanese National | Jōmō-Kōgen–Echigo |
| Gotthard | 14 998 | 1.1.1882[2] | Swiss Federal | Göschenen–Airolo |
| Nakayama | 14 650 | 15.11.1982 | Japanese National | Takasaki–Jōmō-Kōgen |
| Lötschberg | 14 612 | 15.7.1913 | Bern–Lötschberg–Simplon | Goppenstein–Kandersteg |
| Haruna | 14 350 | 15.11.1982 | Japanese National | Takasaki–Jōmō-Kōgen |
| Hokuriku | 13 870 | 10.6.1962 | Japanese National | Maibara–Fukui |
| Mont Cenis (Fréjus) | 13 657 | 17.9.1871 | Italian State | Turin–Modane |
| Shin Shimizu | 13 500 | 15.11.1982 | Japanese National | Takasaki–Niigata |
| Aki | 13 030 | 10.3.1975 | Japanese National | Mihara–Hiroshima |
| Cascade | 12 542 | 12.1.1929 | Burlington Northern, USA | Spokane–Seattle, Washington |
| Flathead | 12 479 | 7.11.1970 | Burlington Northern | Libby–Whitefish, Montana |
| Kitakyushu | 11 747 | 10.3.1975 | Japanese National | Kokura–Hakata |
| Kubiki | 11 353 | 5.1969 | Japanese National | Nou–Nadachi |
| Zao | 11 210 | 23.6.1982 | Japanese National | Fukushima–Shin-Shiroishi |
| Lieråsen | 10 700 | 3.6.1973 | Norwegian State | Oslo–Drammen |
| Santa Lucia | 10 262 | 22.5.1977 | Italian State | Naples–Salerno |
| Arlberg | 10 250 | 20.9.1884 | Austrian Federal | Bludenz–St Anton |

| Name | Length | Date | Operator | Route |
|---|---|---|---|---|
| Moffat | 9 997 | 27.2.1928 | Denver & Rio Grande Western, USA | Denver–Glenwood Springs |
| Ichinoseki | 9 730 | 23.6.1982 | Japanese National | Ichinoseki–Kitakami |
| Orte | 9 371 | 29.4.1980 | Italian State | Rome–Città |
| Kvineshei | 9 064 | 17.12.1943[3] | Norwegian State | Kristiansand–Stavanger |
| Bingo | 8 900 | 10.3.1975 | Japanese National | Fukuyama–Mihara |
| Kaimai | 8 850 | 12.9.1978 | New Zealand Govt | Eaharoa–Apata, North Island |
| Rimutaka | 8 798 | 3.11.1955 | New Zealand Govt | Upper Hutt–Featherston, North Island |
| Uonuma | 8 650 | 15.11.1982 | Japanese National | Urasa–Nagaoka |
| Ricken | 8 603 | 1.10.1910 | Swiss Federal | Wattwil–Uznach |
| Grenchenberg | 8 578 | 1.10.1915 | Swiss Federal[4] | Moutier–Grenchen |
| Otira | 8 563 | 4.8.1923 | New Zealand Govt | Christchurch–Brunner, South Island |
| Tauern | 8 551 | 7.7.1909 | Austrian Federal | Bad Gastein–Spittal |
| Fukuoka | 8 488 | 10.3.1975 | Japanese National | Kokura–Hakata |
| Haegebostad | 8 474 | 17.12.1943[3] | Norwegian State | Kristiansand–Stavanger |
| Ronco | 8 291 | 4.4.1889 | Italian State | Genoa–Milan |
| Hauenstein (new) | 8 134 | 8.1.1916 | Swiss Federal | Tecknau–Olten |
| Tenda | 8 099 | 30.10.1914 | Italian State | Turin–Nice |
| Fukushima | 8 090 | 23.6.1982 | Japanese National | Koriyama–Fukushima |
| Connaught | 8 083 | 6.12.1916 | Canadian Pacific | Field–Revelstoke |
| Karawanken | 7 976 | 1.10.1906 | Austrian Federal | Rosenbach (Austria)–Jesenice (Yugoslavia) |
| Borgallo | 7 972 | 1.8.1894 | Italian State | Parma–La Spezia |
| New Tanna | 7 958 | 1.10.1964 | Japanese National | Tokyo–Shizuoka |
| Somport | 7 874 | 18.7.1928 | French National | Oloran (France)–Jaca (Spain) |

| Tunnel | m | Date | Railway | Position |
|---|---|---|---|---|
| Tanna (Old) | 7 804 | 1.12.1934 | Japanese National | Tokyo–Shizuoka |
| Ulriken | 7 662 | 1.8.1964 | Norwegian State | Bergen–Oslo |
| Hoosac | 7 562 | 9.2.1975 | Boston & Maine, USA | North Adams (Mass) (Boston–Albany) |
| Monte Orso | 7 562 | 28.10.1927 | Italian State | Rome–Naples |
| Lupacino | 7 514 | 24.9.1958 | Italian State | Aulla–Lucca |
| Castiglione | 7 390 | 24.2.1977 | Italian State | Rome–Florence |
| Vivola | 7 355 | 28.10.1927 | Italian State | Rome–Naples |
| Monte Adone | 7 132 | 22.4.1934 | Italian State | Florence–Bologna |
| Jungfrau | 7 123 | 1.8.1912 | Jungfrau, Switzerland | Above Lauterbrunnen |
| Toyohara | 7 030 | 23.6.1982 | Japanese National | Nasu–Shin Shirakawa |
| Severn | 7 011 | 1.9.1886 | British Railways | Swindon–Newport |
| Sainte Marie aux Mines (Lusse) | 6 870 | 9.8.1937 | French National | Saint-Dié–Selestat (converted to road tunnel in July 1973) |
| Shin-Kinmeiji | 6 822 | 10.3.1975 | Japanese National | Shin-Iwakuni–Tokuyama |
| Itsukaichi | 6 640 | 10.3.1975 | Japanese National | Hiroshima–Shin-Iwakuni |
| Ohirayama | 6 585 | 10.3.1975 | Japanese National | Tokuyama–Ogori |
| San Giacomo | 6 514 | 12.5.1977 | Italian State | Savona |
| Marianopoli | 6 475 | 1.8.1885 | Italian State | Valledolmo–Enna, Sicily |
| Tsukiyono | 6 460 | 15.11.1982 | Japanese National | Jōmō-Kogen–Echigo-Yuzawa |
| Turchino | 6 446 | 18.6.1894 | Italian State | Genoa–Asti |
| Wochein (Podbrdo-Bohinj) | 6 339 | 9.7.1906 | Jugoslav State | Jesenice–Nova Gorica |
| Zlatibor | 6 202 | 1.6.1976 | Yugoslav State | Belgrade–Bar |
| Sozina | 6 170 | 1.6.1976 | Yugoslav State | Belgrade–Bar |

| Name | Length (m) | Date | Railway | Route |
|---|---|---|---|---|
| Mont d'Or | 6 097 | 16.5.1915 | French National | Vallorbe (Switzerland) |
| Urasa | 6 020 | 15.11.1982 | Japanese National | Urasa–Nagaoka |
| Col de Braus | 5 949 | 30.10.1928 | French National | Turin–Nice |
| Padornelo | 5 949 | 1959 | Spanish National | Puebla de Sanabria–Carballino |
| Albula | 5 865 | 1.7.1903 | Rhaetian, Switzerland | |
| Gyland | 5 717 | 17.12.1943[3] | Norwegian State | Kristiansand–Stavanger |
| Sant' Oreste | 5 710 | 6.12.1976 | Italian State | Rome–Florence |
| Totley | 5 697 | 6.11.1893[5] | British Railways | Sheffield–Chinley |
| Metropolitana | 5 666 | 28.9.1925 | Italian State | Naples |
| Shin Karikachi | 5 647 | 10.1966 | Japanese National | Ochiai–Shin Karikachi |
| Peloritana | 5 446 | 20.6.1889 | Italian State | Palermo–Messina, Sicily |
| Puymorens | 5 414 | 21.7.1929 | French National | Foix (France)–Puigcerda (Spain) |
| Monte Massico | 5 378 | 28.10.1927 | Italian State | Rome–Naples |
| Senzan | 5 361 | 10.11.1937 | Japanese National | Shikoku |
| Gravehalsen | 5 312 | 10.6.1908 | Norwegian State | Bergen–Oslo |
| Fukasaka | 5 173 | 1.10.1957 | Japanese National | Omi-Shintsu–Shinhikida |
| Biassa II | 5 146 | 14.11.1913 | Italian State | Genoa–La Spezia |
| S Elia-lanculla | 5 142 | 5.12.1960 | Italian State | Reggio Calabria–Brindisi |
| S Cataldo | 5 141 | 30.7.1894 | Italian State | Agropoli–Supri (Naples–Reggio Calabria) |
| Mount Royal | 5 073 | 21.10.1918 | Canadian National | Montreal |
| Ohara | 5 063 | 11.11.1955 | Japanese National | Ohara–Katsuura |
| Otowayama | 5 045 | 1.10.1964 | Japanese National | Tokyo–Osaka |
| Amanus | 4 905 | 1918 | Turkish State | Adana–Aleppo |
| Woodhead New[6] | 4 888 | 14.6.1954 | British Railways | Sheffield–Manchester |
| Standedge[7] | 4 888 | 5.8.1894 | British Railways | Stalybridge–Huddersfield |

see overleaf for notes

**Notes**

[1] Pilot tunnel holed through on 27.1.1983.

[2] For goods traffic; passengers from 1.6.1882.

[3] Wartime opening under German occupation. Full traffic began 1.3.1944.

[4] Grenchenberg Tunnel owned by the Bern–Lötschberg–Simplon Railway but worked by Swiss Federal Railways.

[5] For goods traffic; passengers from 1.6.1894.

[6] Superseded two single-line tunnels 4888 m long opened 23.12.1845 and 2.2.1852. Railway through Woodhead New Tunnel closed 18.7.1981.

[7] Two adjacent single-line bores opened 1.8.1849 and 12.2.1871 were abandoned in October 1966.

The last three tunnels are included because they are nearly 5000 m (over 3 miles) long.

# 16 Railway Bridges over 1000 metres Long

| Bridge | m | ft | Date opened |
|---|---|---|---|
| Huey P. Long, New Orleans, USA | 7 082 | 23 235 | 16.12.1935 |
| Yangtze River, Nanjing, China | 6 772 | 22 218 | 1.10.1968 |
| London–Greenwich | c 6 000 | c 19 000 | 14.12.1836 |
| Hell Gate, New York | 5 862 | 19 233 | 1917 |
| Savannah River, S. Carolina, USA | 3 962 | 13 000 | 1909 |
| Lower Zambezi, Mozambique | 3 678 | 12 064 | 1934 |
| Venice Viaduct, Italy | 3 600 | 11 811 | 1846 |
| Tay, Scotland | 3 552 | 11 653 | 20.6.1887 |
| Storstrøm, Denmark | 3 212 | 10 537 | 26.9.1937 |
| Victoria, Montreal | 3 135 | 10 284 | 13.12.1898[1] |
| Upper Sone, India | 3 064 | 10 052 | 27.2.1900 |
| Ohio River, USA | 3 011 | 9 877 | 1929 |
| Yellow River, Chengchow, China (old) | 3 009 | 9 873 | 11.1905 |
| Yellow River, Chengchow, China (new) | 2 899 | 9 611 | [2] |
| Godavari, India | 2 772 | 9 096 | 6.8.1900 |
| Forth, Scotland | 2 529 | 8 298 | 4.3.1890 |
| Benjamin Franklin, Philadelphia, USA | 2 527 | 8 291 | 4.7.1926 |
| Benjamin Franklin, Philadelphia, USA | 2 527 | 8 291 | 4.7.1926 |
| St Charles, Missouri, USA | 2 400 | 7 876 | 1936 |
| Cairo, Illinois, USA | 2 396 | 7 864 | 1899 |
| Amur, Khabarovsk, USSR | 2 300 | 7 546 | 1916 |
| Newark Bay, New Jersey, USA | 2 259 | 7 411 | 1926 |
| Pont de Cubzac, France | 2 198 | 7 211 | 1886 |
| Mahanadi, India | 2 106 | 6 909 | 11.3.1900 |

RAILWAY BRIDGES OVER 1000 m LONG

| Bridge | m | ft | Date opened |
|---|---|---|---|
| Salado, Santa Fe, Argentina | 2 044 | 6 705 | 1892 |
| Izat, Allahabad, India | 1 945 | 6 381 | 1.1.1905 |
| Havre de Grace, Maryland, USA | 1 877 | 6 108 | 1.1910 |
| Hardinge, Bangladesh | 1 798 | 5 900 | 4.3.1915 |
| Santiago del Estero, Argentina | 1 788 | 5 868 | 1891 |
| Rakaia, South Island, New Zealand | 1 744 | 5 720 | 1939 |
| Martinez—Benicia, California, USA | 1 708 | 5 603 | 1930 |
| Yangtze River, Wuhan, China | 1 670 | 5 479 | 10.1957 |
| Lethbridge Viaduct, Canada | 1 623 | 5 327 | 1909 |
| Ohio River, Louisville, Kentucky, USA | 1 604 | 5 263 | 1918 |
| A. H. Smith Memorial Bridge, Castleton, NY | 1 602 | 5 255 | 1924 |
| Amur River, Baikal—Amur Northern Main Line, USSR | c 1 500 | 4 920 | [3] |
| Lake Pend d'Oreille, near Sanspoint, Idaho, USA | 1 453 | 4 767 | 1902 |
| Batraki, USSR | 1 438 | 4 719 | 1880 |
| Moerdyk, Netherlands | 1 400 | 4 592 | 1880 |
| Ohio River, Pittsburgh, Pennsylvania | 1 388 | 4 555 | 1933 |
| Fuji River, Japan | 1 373 | 4 505 | 1.10.1964 |
| Sacramento River Viaduct, Ca, USA | 1 325 | 4 346 | [3] |
| Memphis, Tennessee, USA | 1 235 | 4 909 | 1917 |
| Yellow River, Tsinan, China | 1 225 | 4 020 | 1911 |
| Ava, Burma | 1 203 | 3 948 | 1934 |
| Yellow River, Fengling Ferry, Shansi, China | 1 194 | 3 918 | [2] |
| Rotterdam Viaduct, Netherlands | 1 180 | 3 870 | [3] |
| Sheyenne River Viaduct, Valley City, North Dakota, USA | 1 177 | 3 863 | 1908 |
| Weldon, North Carolina, USA | 1 165 | 3 822 | 1910 |
| Susquehanna River, Rockville, Pa, USA | 1 161 | 3 808 | 1902 |
| Sydney Harbour, NSW, Australia | 1 149 | 3 770 | 19.3.1932 |
| Zeya River, Baikal—Amur Northern Main line, USSR | c 1 100 | 3 600 | [3] |

| Bridge | m | ft | Date opened |
|--------|-----|-----|-------------|
| Tsien-Tang-Kiang, Hangchow, China | 1 073 | 3 420 | 1937 |
| Upington, South Africa (Orange River) | 1 071 | 3 514 | [3] |
| Harrisburg Viaduct, Pa, USA | 1 069 | 3 507 | [3] |
| Fort Madison, Iowa, USA | 1 020 | 3 347 | 1927 |
| St Louis Bay, USA | 1 015 | 3 330 | 1908 |
| Kiso River, Japan | 1 001 | 3 284 | 1.10.1964 |
| Quebec, Canada (St Lawrence River) | 987 | 3 238 | 3.12.1917 |

[1] Replaced original single-line tubular bridge opened 17.12.1859.
[2] Exact date not known. Altogether there are now ten railway bridges across the Yellow River.
[3] Opening date not known.

Tay Bridge, Dundee, 17 May 1975; 40070 approaching Dundee with a train of tank wagons. The bridge was opened on 20 June 1887. (John Marshall)

The greatest railway bridge in the world, the Forth Bridge near Edinburgh, Scotland, viewed from the south-east. The two main spans each measure 521 m (1710 ft). The double-track railway is carried 47.55 m (156 ft) above high water. The total length of the bridge is 2528 m (8298 ft). The first train crossed on 22 January 1890. (John Marshall)

Forth Bridge – looking north from the top of the north tower, 110 m (361 ft) above the water. A freight train is passing 61 m (200 ft) below. The main upright tubes are 3.65 m (11 ft) in diameter. (John Marshall)

◀ Steelwork of the Forth Bridge, looking south from above Inchgarvie, the island on which the centre tower stands, showing the railway viaduct. (John Marshall)

Müngstener Bridge, highest in Germany, built in 1897, carrying a double-track railway 107 m (350 ft) above the River Wupper near Solingen, with a span of 160 m (525 ft). (John Marshall)

Freight train crossing Bietschtal Bridge, Bern–Lötschberg–Simplon Railway, Switzerland, on 29 July 1966. (John Marshall)

Pfaffenberg–Zwenberg bridge, Tauern Railway, Austria, opened on 30 July 1971. The world's largest concrete arch railway bridge; span 200 m (660 ft), height 120 m (394 ft). (John Marshall)

# 17 Bibliography

The sheer quantity of railway literature is now so vast that the number of books published in Great Britain alone is beyond the capacity of the ordinary person to absorb. The best guide to selection is the monumental *Bibliography of British Railway History* by George Ottley. This first appeared in 1965 and was republished in 1983 by Her Majesty's Stationery Office (ISBN 0-11-290334-7). A supplementary volume, bringing the work up to date, is to be published by HMSO in 1985.

Much of the information in this Guinness publication was obtained from Year Books of statistics published by various countries: Australia, Canada, China, USSR and others. Some countries, such as USA, Japan, and France, publish annual books of railway facts and statistics.

The principal publishers of railway books in Britain are Ian Allan of Shepperton, Surrey; George Allen & Unwin of London; David & Charles of Newton Abbot, Devon; Oakwood Press of Blandford, Dorset; and The Oxford Publishing Company, now Blandford Press of Poole, Dorset. It is worth obtaining their current catalogues. The Railway Correspondence & Travel Society publish excellent locomotive histories chiefly of the Great Western, London & North Eastern and the Southern companies.

In North America many railway books are published by Bonanza Books, New York; Howell North, Berkeley, California; and Kalmbach Publishing Company, Milwaukee, Wisconsin.

Adequate histories of most of the larger British railway companies have been published, with the notable exception of the Caledonian and the London & North Western. The following are outstanding:

Barker, T. G. & Robbins, M. A. *A History of London Transport*, George Allen & Unwin, 2 vols 1963, 1974 ISBN 0-04-385063-4

Dow, G. *Great Central*, Ian Allan, 3 vols 1959, 1962, 1965

Grinling, C. *The History of the Great Northern Railway* (1903), George Allen & Unwin, 1966

Macdermot, E. T. *History of the Great Western Railway* (1927), Ian Allan, 2 vols 1964

BIBLIOGRAPHY

Tomlinson, W. W. *The North Eastern Railway* (1915), David & Charles, 1967

Beside the titles listed below there are numerous books on small railway companies and exhaustive studies of short sections of line and branches, and of various locomotive types.

## General Reference

Awdry, W.; Cook, C. (Eds) *A Guide to the Steam Railways of Great Britain*, Pelham Books, 1984, ISBN 0-7207-14176

Baker, S. K. *Rail Atlas of Britain*, Oxford Publishing Co, 1980, ISBN 0-86093-1064

Borley, H. V. *Chronology of London Railways*, Railway & Canal Historical Society, 1982, ISBN 0-901461-33-4

*Bradshaw's Railway Manual and Shareholders' Guide and Directory* (1869), David & Charles, 1969, ISBN 0-7153-4358-0

*British Rail Atlas*, Ian Allan, 1967

*British Rail Main Line Gradient Profiles*, Ian Allan, no date

Clinker, C. R. *Register of closed Passenger Stations and Goods Depots in England, Scotland and Wales 1830–1977*, Avon Anglia, 1978, ISBN 0-905466-19-5

Cook, R. A. *Historical Maps*, Railway & Canal Historical Society. *Lancashire & Yorkshire Railway* 1976, SBN 901461-20-2; *North Eastern Railway* 1975, SBN 901461-10-5; *Great North of Scotland and Highland Railways* 1977, SBN 901461-22-9

James, L. *A Chronology of the construction of Britain's Railways 1778–1885*, Ian Allan 1983, ISBN 0-7110-1277-6

Jane's *World Railways*, Jane's, Annual

Jane's *Urban Transport Systems*, Jane's, Annual

Marshall, J. *A Biographical Dictionary of Railway Engineers*, David & Charles 1978, ISBN 0-7153-7489-3

Marshall, J. *The Guinness Book of Rail Facts and Feats*, 3rd Edition, Guinness Superlatives Ltd, 1979, ISBN 0-900424-56-7

*Railway Directory & Year Book*, Annual, IPC Transport Press

*Railway Junction Diagrams 1915*, (Railway Clearing House), David & Charles, 1969, ISBN 0-7153-4347-5. (A similar book is now published by Ian Allan)

Wignall, C. J. *Complete British Railways Maps and Gazetteer from 1830 to 1987*, Oxford Publishing Co, 1983, ISBN 0-86093-162-5

## Railway History

Acworth, W. M. *The Railways of England* (5th Edition 1900), Ian Allan, 1964

Berton, P. *The Great Railway* (History of the Canadian Pacific Railway), McClelland & Stewart, Toronto. Vol 1 *The National Dream*, 1970, ISBN 0-7710-1326-4; Vol 2, 1971, ISBN 0-7710-1327-2

Burgess, G. H.; Kennedy, M. C. *Centennial History of the Pennsylvania Railroad Co 1846–1946*, Pennsylvania RR Co, 1949

Ellis, H. *Nineteenth Century Railway Carriages*, Modern Transport, 1949

Kichenside, G. M. *Railway Carriage Album*, Ian Allan, 1980, ISBN 0-7110-1058-7

Lavallee, O. *Van Horne's Road*, (Canadian Pacific Railway), Railfare Enterprises, Montreal, 1974, ISBN 0-919130-22-4

Lewin, H. G. *Early British Railways*, Locomotive Publishing Co, 1925

Lewin, H. G. *The Railway Mania and its aftermath 1845–52* (1936), David & Charles, 1968, ISBN 0-7153-4262-2

Lewis, M. J. T. *Early wooden railways*, Routledge & Kegan Paul, 1970, ISBN 0-7100-7818-8

Pratt, E. A. *A History of Inland Transport and Communication* (1912), David & Charles, 1970, SBN 7153-4703-9

Priestley, J. *Navigable Rivers, Canals and Railways* (1831), David & Charles, 1969, SBN 7153-4395-5

Robbins, M. *The Railway Age*, Routledge & Kegan Paul, 1962

Simmons, J. *The Railways of Britain, an Historical Survey*, Routledge & Kegan Paul, 1961

Stover, J. F. *American Railroads*, University of Chicago Press, 1961

Whishaw, F. *Railways of Great Britain and Ireland* (1842), David & Charles, 1969, SBN 7153-4786-1

*A Regional History of the Railways of Great Britain*, A series of 15 volumes published by David & Charles:
Vol 1 Thomas, D. St J. *The West Country*, 5th Edn, 1981, ISBN 0-7153-8152-0
Vol 2 White, H. P. *Southern England*, 4th Edn, 1982, ISBN 0-7153-8365-5
Vol 3 White, H. P. *Greater London*, 1963, ISBN 0-7153-5337-3
Vol 4 Hoole, K. *North East England*, 1978, ISBN 0-7153-7746-9
Vol 5 Gordon, D. I. *The Eastern Counties*, 1977, ISBN 0-7153-7431-1
Vol 6 Thomas, J. *Scotland, Lowlands and Borders*, 1971, ISBN 0-7153-5408-6
Vol 7 Christiansen, R. *The West Midlands*, 1973, ISBN 0-7153-6093-0
Vol 8 Joy, D. *South and West Yorkshire*, 1975, ISBN 0-7153-6883-4

Vol 9 Leleux, R. *The East Midlands*, 1976, ISBN 0-7153-7165-7

Vol 10 Holt, G. O. *The North West*, 1978, ISBN 0-7153-7521-0

Vol 11 Baughan, P. E. *North and Mid Wales*, 1980, ISBN 0-7153-7850-3

Vol 12 Barrie, D. S. M. *South Wales*, 1980, ISBN 0-7153-7970-4

Vol 13 Christiansen, R. *Thames and Severn*, 1981, ISBN 0-7153-8004-4

Vol 14 Joy, D. *The Lake Counties*, 1983, ISBN 0-946537-02-X

Vol 15 Paterson, A. J. *Scotland, The East Coast and Highlands* Not yet published

*Railroads of America* Series published by Macmillan, New York:

Brewer, T. B.; Dickes, A. *The Missouri Pacific*

Bryant, K. *The Atcheson, Topeka & Santa Fe*

Catton, W. *The Baltimore & Ohio*

Klein, M. *The Louisville & Nashville*, 1972

Lamb, W. K. *The Canadian Pacific*

Peterson, R. L. *The Northern Pacific*

Stevens, G. R. *The Canadian National*, 1973

Stover, J. F. *The Illinois Central*

## Locomotive History

Ahrons, E. L. *The British Steam Railway Locomotive 1825–1925*, Locomotive Publishing Co, 1927, 1961

Brownlie, J. S. *Railway Steam Cranes*, Published by the author, 1973, ISBN 0-9502965-0-3

Bruce, A. W. *The Steam Locomotive in America*, Norton & Co, New York, 1952

Cook, A. F.; Hollingsworth, B. *The Illustrated Encyclopaedia of the World's Modern Locomotives*, Salamander Books Ltd, 1983, ISBN 0-86101-176-7

Hollingsworth, B. *The Illustrated Encyclopaedia of North American Locomotives*, Salamander Books, 1983, ISBN 0-86101-148-1

Jones, K. P. *Steam Locomotive Development 1923–1962* (A critical bibliography), Library Association, 1969, SBN 85365

*Locomotive Cyclopaedia of American Practice*, 1925, Newton K. Gregg, California, 1973, ISBN 0-912318-38-4

Lowe, J. W. *British Steam Locomotive Builders*, Goose & Son, 1975, ISBN 0-900404-21-3

Railway Correspondence & Travel Society Locomotive Histories: Great Western Railway; London & North Eastern Railway; London & South Western Railway; London, Brighton & South Coast Railway; London, Chatham & Dover Railway; South Eastern Railway; South Eastern & Chatham Railway; Southern Railway

Ransome Wallis, P. (Ed) *The Concise Encyclopaedia of World Railway Locomotives*, Hutchinson, 1959

Sinclair, A. *Development of the Locomotive Engine* (1907), MIT Press, 1970, ISBN 0-262-19068-0

Warren, J. G. H. *A Century of Locomotive Building by Robert Stephenson & Co* (1923), David & Charles, 1970, SBN 7153-4378-5

Westing, F. *The Locomotives that Baldwin built*, Bonanza Books, N.Y., 1966

White, J. H. Jr *American Locomotives, An Engineering History, 1830–1880*, John Hopkins Press, Baltimore, Md, 1968

Wiener, L. *Articulated Locomotives* (1930), Kalmbach Publishing Co, Milwaukee, Wisconsin, 1970

## Technical

Cooper, B. K. *British Rail Handbook*, Ian Allan, 1981, ISBN 0-7110-1027-7

Harvey, D. W. *A Manual of Steam Locomotive Restoration and Preservation*, David & Charles, 1980, ISBN 0-7153-7770-1

Kichenside, G. M.; Williams, A. *British Railway Signalling*, Ian Allan, 1978, ISBN 0-7110-0898-1

Mann, F. A. W. *Railway Bridge Construction*, Hutchinson Education, 1972, ISBN 0-09-108630-2

Nock, O. S. *Fifty Years of Railway Signalling*, Institution of Railway Signal Engineers (Ian Allan), 1962

Schneider, A. *Railways through the Mountains of Europe*, Ian Allan, 1967

# Index